THE AGE OF
IMPERIALISM

Harry Magdoff

THE AGE OF IMPERIALISM

The Economics of U.S. Foreign Policy

Modern Reader Paperbacks
New York and London

To Beatrice
for the best of reasons

Library of Congress Catalog Card Number: 69-19788

First Modern Reader Paperback Edition 1969
Tenth Printing

Chapters 2, 3, 4, and 5 originally appeared
in *Monthly Review* in June 1968, October 1968,
November 1968, and November 1966

Published by Monthly Review Press
62 West 14th Street, New York, N.Y. 10011
21 Theobalds Road, London WC1X 8SL

Manufactured in the United States of America

Contents

1

INTRODUCTION

The essays presented here were written in response to questions asked repeatedly during and after lectures given at various colleges.

Bewildered by the fury, irrationality, and horror of the escalation of the war in Vietnam, many students began to probe for causes: Is the war part of a more general and consistent scheme of United States external policies or is it an aberration of a particular group of men in power?

Brushing aside propagandistic arguments about higher morality and a threat to national security, inquiring students were inclined to seek hidden motives. Perhaps, some thought, there were vital raw materials or exceptional business opportunities in South Vietnam that might explain the intensity and single-mindedness of the United States government's headlong course of conquest. Finding no clear-cut or adequate answers along this line, some were led to attempt a more general assessment of the situation in Southeast Asia. From this came the hypothesis that the Vietnam War was part of a more general United States strategy composed of several elements:

(1) A United States drive to control and influence all of Southeast Asia, an area containing over 200 million souls and one and a half million square miles of territory. Here, the stake of markets and raw material sources (potential as well as current) is significant not only for the United States but also for an industrialized Japan that could function as a junior partner in the United States empire.

7

(2) A military decision to establish a strong and reliable base in South Vietnam, where huge stores of equipment and supplies could be accumulated and military manpower stationed.

(3) Use of such a military base, on or near the coast and close to North Vietnam, as a source of power not only for control and influence over all of Southeast Asia, but also as part of an iron ring around the People's Republic of China and the Democratic Republic of Vietnam. This would serve not only as a threat but as a staging area in case of a land war against Asian communist countries.

This type of thinking, considered against the history of the Cold War, led the more sophisticated to a broader area of inquiry: Is the tap-root of United States policy perhaps to be found in a modern imperialism, in capitalism as an expansionist system? But here they were stumped again. The imperialism hypothesis seemed to be in conflict with the commonly accepted notion that exports and foreign investments are minor elements in the overall U.S. economy.[1] Could this apparent contradiction be resolved?

Here the existing economic literature was not of much help. It is true that economists have in recent years been paying more attention to international economic affairs, especially on such matters as the balance of payments, gold, foreign aid, international trade, and the problems of underdeveloped countries. Nevertheless, apart from a growing literature on the legal and administrative aspects of international business investment which is mainly concerned with practical business matters, very little study has been devoted to the relation between the domestic and international economies. Economic theorists as a rule have refrained from analyzing the United States as a world economic power or studying the country as part of the world capitalist system.

A striking example of the way this issue is side-stepped is provided by John Kenneth Galbraith's magnum opus, *The New Industrial State*. Here Galbraith boldly attempts to break new ground and is not inhibited by accepted orthodoxy from arriving at new theoretical generalizations. Since the pivot of his analysis is the concept of a U.S. economy dominated by giant corporations, he stresses again and again their strategic influence on economic and political affairs, and the imperative need of these corporations, for their own safety and protection, to control their sources of raw materials and their markets. Yet one would never know from Galbraith's book that these corporations have any foreign economic interests, despite the fact, documented below, that foreign sources of raw materials and foreign markets for their products are a significant and growing component of the business activity of the giant corporations. Not only is this aspect ignored in Galbraith's treatment of the corporation, but it is ignored also in his discussion of the relationship between corporate interests and foreign military policy. On the latter, he emphasizes the strategic role of military expenditures in the growth and security of the giant firms. But one will not find a word on the foreign involvement of the giant corporations—even though Galbraith's theoretical framework, built around the imperatives of corporate control over raw materials and markets, cries out for such an analysis.

The repeated questions of students about the anomaly of an "isolationist" economy and an aggressive international foreign policy reflected the absence of such inquiries by orthodox scholars or even by liberal and radical social critics. It was both the significance of the questions posed and the scholarly vacuum which prompted the studies published here. An invitation to give a paper on imperialism to the second Socialist Scholars Conference held in New York in September, 1966, provided the occasion for presenting publicly the first results of the search for an answer to this question. (A revised version of this paper, published in the November, 1966, issue of *Monthly Review*, is reprinted here as Chapter V.)

The primary task was to gather and evaluate enough facts to test the almost universal assumption that foreign economic activities are a small, even insignificant, element in U.S. business interests. What do these facts show? The answer, it seems to me, is unambiguous: the prevailing assumptions are false. The crux of the matter is a general failure to recognize the full im-

pact of foreign investments, to understand that while the export
of capital in the form of direct investment—in mines, oil wells,
and manufacturing—is much smaller than exports in any given
year, the cumulative effect of the annual flow of investment results in an economic involvement that is much greater by far
than exports.

When one takes into account, as is customary, only the
annual amounts of commodity and capital exports, the effect
of the accumulation of foreign investments is overlooked. Exports of commodities, in contrast with exports of capital, represent only a *flow*: businessmen seek to maintain and increase
this flow from the output of plants located in the United States.
The flow has to be renewed each year: last year's flow abroad
belongs to the past; new sales must be sought for this year's
product.

Investments moving abroad, in contrast, build up a *stock*
of investments. An investment in plant and equipment abroad
remains abroad forever and ever, unless the entire enterprise is
eventually sold, confiscated, or as in the case of minerals, until
the natural resource is finally exhausted. But as long as the
business investment exists abroad and there are markets for its
products, the investment is self-perpetuating. The prices of the
products sold include, in addition to profits and the costs of
labor and raw materials, depreciation of capital (or depletion
of reserves). Thus funds are continuously generated not only
for "eternal" profits but also "eternal" replacement of used-up
equipment and/or the exploitation of new mineral sources. And
of course each new investment flowing abroad adds to the
"permanent" *stock* of investment.

A simple arithmetic illustration may help to explain this
point. Assume that U.S. corporations invest $5 billion abroad
each year. Assume, further, that for every $5 billion of invest-
ment it is reasonable to expect $10 billion of product (or $2 of
product manufactured each year with $1 of initial investment
in plant and equipment). Then we would get the following
results:

Year	Annual Flow of Capital Invested Abroad	Accumulated Stock of Capital Abroad at End of Year	Annual Output Resulting from Use of Capital Equipment
		— In Billions of Dollars —	
1	5	5	10
2	5	10	20
3	5	15	30
.	.	.	.
.	.	.	.
.	.	.	.
10	5	50	100

Thus, the first year's investment would produce a stock of $5 billion, from which $10 billion of products are available for sale each year. In the second year, the additional flow of $5 billion would be added to the previous year's investment. Now we have an accumulated stock of $10 billion. This is plant and equipment with which $20 billion of new products can be produced annually. By the tenth year, the accumulated stock reaches an investment of $50 billion, and the annual marketable production becomes $100 billion.

Here we can see that if one speaks of the relatively small amount of investments flowing abroad each year, one misses the full meaning of the accumulated impact of such investment activity. It follows that if one looks only at the annual volume of commodity and capital exports each year, the full impact of United States business abroad is disregarded. Assume that the annual flow of United States exports amounts to $25 billion and compare this with the results of ten years of foreign investment at the annual rate of $5 billion, as shown in our illustration: the annual foreign business resulting from the accumulated stock of investment amounts to $100 billion, or four times exports.

This way of looking at U.S. foreign business adds a new dimension to our understanding of the extent of the country's foreign economic involvement, providing the framework for the examination in what follows of the magnitude of foreign sales, investment, and the flow of profits resulting from these investments.

But our interest is not only in the size of foreign economic involvements; it is also necessary to ask how important these activities are for the domestic economy. If we think in terms of an arithmetic ratio, we can see that thus far we have been discussing only the numerator. What do we use for a denominator? Here again, we encounter a widespread shortcoming in the commonly accepted way of thinking about such matters. A customary way of measuring significance in economic affairs is to compare variables under examination with the Gross National Product (GNP). If a particular segment of the economy measures up as a large proportion of the GNP, it is *ipso facto* assumed to be important. Conversely, if the ratio to the GNP is small, then the particular item measured is usually considered not important.

The weakness of this type of statistical test is that it does not differentiate between the strategic and the non-strategic sectors of the economy, between the dependent and the independent variables, between the activities that create a surplus product and those that are involved in utilizing the surplus. (For an understanding of this question, the reader should consult Paul A. Baran and Paul M. Sweezy, *Monopoly Capital*, New York, 1966.) Here it is sufficient to note that the procedure followed was to narrow down the base for evaluating the relative significance of foreign economic activity so that the latter was correlated with comparable sectors of the domestic economy. In addition, special account was taken of such strategic sectors as the capital goods industries, which are the most volatile elements in the business cycle.

The resulting analysis of the available facts shows that there is a close parallel between, on the one hand, the aggressive United States foreign policy aimed at controlling (directly and indirectly) as much of the globe as possible, and, on the other hand, an energetic international expansionist policy of U.S. business. The demonstration of this parallel of course does not prove that one is the cause of the other. What it does suggest is that it is simply wrong to assume that the U.S. economy is "isolationist," and from this it follows that the spread of U.S. international economic affairs has to be introduced as an important consideration in any hypotheses attempting to explain what goes on in the world today.

In order to understand the main past and potential future trends, we need to sort out the more important influences from the multitude of variables. However, attempting to arrive at a simple, single-cause formula more often than not serves as a strait jacket on the advance of knowledge. In the case of imperialism, we have, at one extreme, theorists who look to some universal in man's nature or to a form of social atavism to explain the phenomenon as a continuous and constant force in history. Thus, we have so competent an economic historian as Professor David S. Landes explaining:

It seems to me that one has to look at imperialism as a multifarious response to a common opportunity that consists simply in disparity of power. Whenever and wherever such disparity has existed, people and groups have been ready to take advantage of it. It is, one notes with regret, in the nature of the human beast to push other people around—or to save their souls or "civilize" them, as the case may be.[2]

This interpretation, correct or incorrect, is at so high a level of abstraction that it contributes nothing to an understanding of historical differences in types and purposes of aggression and expansion. It is entirely irrelevant, for example, to an explanation of the historical expansion of capitalist society into a world system, or of why this expansion is associated with a growing disparity of power between a few nations that are exceptionally rich and many nations that are continuously poor.

At the other extreme of the oversimplication spectrum is the "pure" economic imperialism formula. The search for unadulterated economic motives of foreign policy decisions will serve as a useful hypothesis in a large number of cases. But it will fail if one expects to find such for *each and every* act of political and military policy.

A major reason why such a crude hypothesis does not work is simply that military and political policies are not based on strict cost-accounting rules. The corporation does need to weigh carefully every expenditure of funds against the prospect of re-

covering the funds and making a sought-for profit in a reasonable period of time. Governments, on the other hand, are not
restricted by the same kind of budgetary considerations: they
can tax, print money, and raise the public debt. There are of
course limits even to these expenditures, but they arise from the
resources of the whole economy and not from those of a given
corporation or a group of corporations.

The rationale of government spending has no resemblance
to the rigid weighing of costs versus benefits, even though some
governments may wish to have it appear that they do. A government can spend billions (with revenue collected from the population as a whole) to dominate a banana-producing country
even though the resulting control protects profits in the millions
for only one or two corporations. But the reality of imperialism
goes far beyond the immediate interest of this or that investor:
the underlying purpose is nothing less than keeping as much as
possible of the world open for trade and investment by the giant
multinational corporations. Where there are competing interests
between the business organizations of different countries, the
aim of each government's policy is to keep on extending its foreign influence. The dimension of the control will vary, from military occupation to informal spheres-of-influence techniques, depending on circumstances and the judgment of political and
military leaders on what is most realistic under the circumstances.

When all these factors are taken into account, it will be seen
that attempts to explain isolated actions in "bookkeeping" terms
make no sense. Small Latin American countries that produce
relatively little profit are important in United States policy-mak-
ing because control over all of Latin America is important. Control and influence, in this context, are needed not only to prevent
expropriation of U.S. capital and to immunize the country
against social revolution, but even because its vote in the UN
or the OAS is important to the general U.S. scheme of domination. Understood in these terms, the killing and destruction in
Vietnam and the expenditure of vast sums of money are not
balanced in the eyes of U.S. policy makers against profitable
business opportunities in Vietnam; rather they are weighed according to the judgment of military and political leaders on

what is necessary to control and influence Asia, and especially Southeast Asia, in order to keep the entire area within the imperialist system in general, and within the United States sphere of influence in particular.

The same type of thinking that approaches the concept of economic imperialism in the restricted balance-sheet sense usually also confines the term to control (direct or indirect) by an industrial power over an underdeveloped country. Such a limitation ignores the essential feature of the new imperialism that arises in the late nineteenth century: the competitive struggle among the industrial nations for dominant positions with respect to the *world* market and raw material sources.

The structural difference which distinguishes the new imperialism from the old is the replacement of an economy in which many firms compete by one in which a handful of giant corporations in each industry compete. Further, during this period, the advance of transportation and communication technology and the challenge to England by the newer industrial nations brought two additional features to the imperialist stage: an intensification of competitive struggle in the world arena and the maturation of a truly international capitalist system. Under these circumstances, the competition among groups of giant corporations and their governments takes place over the entire globe: in the markets of the advanced nations as well as in those of the semi-industrialized and non-industrialized nations. The struggle for power by the industrialized nations for colonial and informal control over the economically backward regions is but one phase of this economic war and only one attribute of the new imperialism.

The nations in the world capitalist system have varying degrees of strength and independence, and the jockeying for power and control extends throughout the system—among the big as well as the small, among the relatively rich as well as among the relatively poor. Circumscribing imperialism to merely operations in the underdeveloped world is indeed strange when one considers the consistency of Germany's aims with respect to other European nations during two world wars: a program to reorganize and control *industrialized* as well as *non-indus-trialized* nations to serve the needs of an expanding German capitalism.

Nowadays it is frequently said that the greater involvement by United States capital in Western Europe, as contrasted with investments in the underdeveloped countries, is evidence of a departure from imperialism. This view is of course untenable if one recognizes that antagonism between unevenly developing industrial centers is the hub of the imperialist wheel.

But there is an additional perspective with which U.S. capital expansion in other advanced nations should be viewed. The higher standard of living and the great amount of capital accumulated in Western Europe are rooted in past and present advantages obtained by the latter area through exploitation of colonial and neo-colonial countries. By penetrating the metro-politan centers of Europe, U.S. capital skims off part of the cream: it benefits from (a) the enlarged consumer markets of Western Europe and (b) the opportunity to trade through chan-nels developed by the metropolitan centers in their relations with their dependencies. Here an analogy with the days of piracy may help, when certain entrepreneurs made their living by prey-ing on the wealth of islands and coasts far from the metropolitan centers. Now, imagine an entrepreneur who outfits a ship for the purpose of hijacking pirate ships that are returning to the home country. Is the investment in the latter enterprise any less dependent on piracy than that of the original pirate? In this sense, it should be noted that the extensive investment by the U.S. petroleum industry in West Europe (see Chapter II, Table XIII) obtains its profits by refining and distributing oil im-ported from the Middle East.

Exaggerations of the economic imperialism theory are not restricted to its advocates. The more ludicrous versions of mechanistic analysis of economic imperialism are to be found in the writings of critics. An outstanding example of this occurs in an essay by Professor Mark Blaug on "Economic Imperialism Revisited." Among other things, Professor Blaug submits what he considers to be a devastating refutation of the notion that export of capital is induced by greater profit opportunities abroad:

Arabian

What is even more striking is that rates of return on foreign investment in the ~~Persian~~ Gulf are as high as 20 percent in contrast to the 11 percent in Latin America and 8 percent in Canada; yet the Persian Gulf attracts less than one tenth of American foreign investment and the rate of increase of foreign investment in the postwar years has been higher in Canada than in the oil-soaked regions of the Middle East.[3]

Here we see the formula mentality in full bloom. Despite appearances, the argument has no resemblance to the reality of business behavior. The fact that profits from oil investments in the Persian Gulf are so high hardly means that an additional unit of investment will create an equivalent return of profit. Once a given source of oil is tapped and the most efficient arrangement of wells is achieved, further desirable investment opportunities are quite limited (other than investments to preclude competitors from getting hold of oil reserves). After a certain point is reached, additional investment would not yield the desired rate of return. This constraint on further investment is particularly pronounced when, as in the oil industry, there is such a high degree of concentration of ownership of oil leases. This sort of elementary business consideration applies to many situations. Thus, once a railroad line is built, absorbing all the available freight and passenger traffic between two points, the addition of lines would be fruitless no matter how profitable the original investment may be.

Professor Blaug was apparently more interested in denying the existence of imperialism than in trying to understand its nature. If he had been interested in exploring the significance of the facts he cited, he would have addressed himself to such questions as: Why is it that there are not significant profitable opportunities for U.S. capital in the Persian Gulf other than in oil? Why is it that a region that can produce such huge profits does not have large enough consumer markets to support other profitable investments?

Another illustration of distortion by use of unassimilated, or unanalyzed, facts is found in a chapter labelled "Is America Imperialist?" in Barbara Ward's *The West at Bay*. Among reasons given to disprove the notion that the United States is imperialist, Miss Ward observes: "In the past, Americans have not sought to break deadlocks at home by conquering new markets abroad. On the contrary, they have cut lending and foreign trading to the bone."[4]

The first sentence is of course dead wrong and is contradicted by the entire course of United States economic history.[5] Still, Miss Ward does present data to support her argument. And this is what she submits: during the depression years, from 1929 to 1933, exports of merchandise declined from $5.2 to $1.6 billion, and foreign lending declined from $2.7 to $0.4 billion.

But surely these data do not substantiate the claim that the United States "cut lending and foreign trade to the bone." The reduction in foreign trade and investment was not voluntary. Counter-measures to resuscitate foreign trade were vigorously pursued, but they were impotent in face of the severity of the depression. The reality of the early 1930's was a collapse of international trade: a failure of the world capitalist system which neither capitalists nor governments were able to prevent. Foreign lending shrank because there were very few reliable borrowers: over $22 billion of foreign public debt was in default in those years. Similarly, there was no basis for maintaining, let alone increasing, export trade. Businessmen do not export unless there are foreign customers who have the wherewithal to pay for their purchases. Such customers did not exist in a period of world-wide depression complicated by a disintegration of the international payments system.

These two examples by no means exhaust the various fallacies found in the literature on imperialism. They were deliberately selected because they are in some ways representative of the kinds of difficulties students, advanced as well as elementary, face in dealing with economic theory as contrasted with economic practice. When discussing theory we deal with abstractions and try to isolate the most important forces making for change and development. But in real life these forces are intermingled with many others. The real task in economic analysis is to move intelligently and comfortably back and forth— from abstract theory to concrete reality and vice versa. Serious difficulties arise if the leap between the abstract and the concrete is too sudden and too extreme, without proper attention to the intermediate stages of analysis.

As an illustration, let us look at the profit motive as a regulator of business activity. There can be little question that the drive for higher profit rates and a larger volume of profits is the propelling force of business enterprise. Yet this most valid and essential generalization has different applications according to circumstances. Business profit strategy will vary between industries, between periods of prosperity and periods of depression, and between competitive and monopolistic situations. On the question of foreign investment by United States business, it is important to recognize the influence of the need by monopolistic-type firms to control raw material sources and markets in order to protect their dominant position and to secure their investment. Even in this context some firms, because of the nature of their business, will adopt a relatively longer-run profit perspective, while others will invest abroad only if they can recoup their capital in three to five years. The common thread in these various strategies is, of course, growth of profits. Nevertheless, one would get a misleading picture if one narrowed down the reasons for the migration of capital to merely a statistical analysis of profit rate differentials in various countries.

Similar strictures need to be applied to the surplus capital themes that are often found in theories of imperialism. It seems almost axiomatic to say that capital moves abroad when idle funds that find no profitable domestic investment outlets and/or profit opportunities are greater abroad than at home. This abstraction is a useful first approximation, a starting point and a guide for investigation, but by no means an adequate explanation for the many different types of capital movement. Capital in everyday life is not an undifferentiated mass. It is supplied from different sources in the economy and is frequently available for only limited uses—a short-term loan, opening a new bank, building a chemical plant. It should also be understood that money capital consists of credit as well as cash and therefore is affected by the swings of the credit cycle. Thus during a severe depression, as production declines and credit contracts, a good part of the surplus disappears and mobilization of capital becomes more difficult.

The often-repeated theorem about foreign investment as a way out of depression has validity if one recognizes that this is only one of the strategies on the agenda of the business community, which may or may not be workable according to circumstances. If a depression is worldwide and the international credit system has collapsed, foreign investment as an option will generally disappear from the agenda except as it may be feasible to grab off some valuable mineral resource or buy up a weaker competitor.

During the upward swing of the cycle, the appearance of surplus capacity in domestic production raises the issue of finding foreign outlets for idle capital; the successful pursuit of these foreign outlets may help to prolong the upward swing. This applies not only to the cycle as a whole but to the cycles of individual industries as well. An example of the latter is the shift of Engish, United States, French, and German capital connected with the railway industry from one country to another. When the practical limit of railroad building was being reached in one country, outlets in another country were sought. The pursuit was intensified as competition increased among the capital-exporting countries.

What matters to the business community, and to the business system as a whole, is that the option of foreign investment (and foreign trade) should remain available. For this to be meaningful, the business system requires, as a minimum, that the political and economic principles of capitalism should prevail and that the door be fully open for foreign capital at all times. Even more, it seeks a privileged open door for the capital of the home country in preference to capital from competing industrial nations. How much or how little an open door may be exploited at any given time is not the issue. The *principle* must be maintained, especially for a capitalist super-power like the United States, and especially when it is being challenged widely and openly. (In addition, who knows when some vital resource will be discovered and the particular open door will lead to a source of new treasure?)

Maintaining the open door creates problems, some because of conflicting interests among the more mature capitalist nations, some because of the actual and potential social revolutions which threaten to eliminate (or limit) capitalism and freedom for private investment and trade. Hence, opening the door and keeping it open require eternal vigilance and will power. What is needed, in other words, is the strength and persistence on the part of the more advanced nations to influence and control the politics and economics of the less advanced nations. Since outright colonial possession has in the main become impractical, other means—some traditional, some new—are being explored and exploited. In this, the United States is the major practitioner, having seized the opportunity at the end of the Second World War to organize and dominate the imperialist network.

Traditional means are still available and in use. The method of invasion and the exercise of military force is still with us; only the rationalizations are updated. A globe-straddling navy and an extensive network of military bases weigh heavily on the rest of the world. Much reliance is placed on newer techniques, not entirely new but applied on a vaster scale and with greater sophistication than in the past: military assistance to bolster "reliable" governments against revolution; economic aid to induce an environment hospitable to foreign capital and imports; and then there is the ubiquitous CIA. The objective underpinning of the system of alliances and control remains the market and financial relations which reproduce the economic dependence of the less advanced regions on the metropolitan centers.

Seen in this light, there is no fundamental conflict between economic, political, and military interests. Differences do and will exist due to opposing interests among business groups, special interests of other social classes and strata, and bureaucratic concerns of government officials and the military elite. But the resulting discord is concerned with the choice of strategy and tactics on how best to assure the growth and expansion of the business system, how best to keep as much of the world free for private enterprise and especially for that of the United States.

To get a better understanding of all this, it is necessary to study the historic origins of the imperialist system and to identify the interrelationship between various aspects of the economic and financial structure of the United States on the one hand and the international economic activity of business and government on the other. This was the framework of a paper presented to the third Socialist Scholars Conference (New York, September, 1967), on the occasion of the 50th anniversary of the publication of Lenin's *Imperialism, The Highest Stage of Capitalism*. A greatly expanded version of this paper was published in the June, October, and November, 1968, issues of *Monthly Review* and is reprinted here as Chapters II, III, and IV. The major purpose of these chapters is to show the cohesion and interdependence of the United States economy and the world capitalist system. The contradictions and tensions within the system are referred to only incidentally. No attempt has been made to subject to analysis either the conflicts between rivals within the system or the revolutionary surge to weaken and eliminate imperialism. These essays should therefore be considered as an introduction to the study of United States imperialism—providing, hopefully, a more significant framework than is currently available for understanding the question and a point of departure for further investigation.

Once one comprehends the interdependence of the international and domestic economic structures, one can begin to recognize the limited alternatives under which the administrators of the business system operate. Students are not alone in assuming that there is an almost limitless range of alternatives available to a democratic political system, so that with reason, imagination, and good will capitalism can pursue its course without imperialism. An interesting illustration of the thought processes involved in the "free will," or limitless-alternative, approach is to be found in J. A. Hobson's important book on imperialism, written in 1902:

There is no necessity to open up new markets; the home

markets are capable of indefinite expansion. Whatever is produced in England can be consumed in England, provided that the "income" or power to demand commodities, is properly distributed. This only appears untrue because of the unnatural and unwholesome specialization to which this country has been subjected, based upon a bad distribution of economic resources, which has induced an overgrowth of certain manufacturing trades for the express purpose of effecting foreign sales. If the industrial revolution had taken place in an England founded upon equal access by all classes to land, education and legislation, specialization in manufactures would not have gone so far (though more intelligent progress would have been made, by reason of a widening of the area of selection of inventive and organizing talents) ; foreign trade would have been less important, though more steady; the standard of life for all portions of the population would have been high, and the present rate of national consumption would probably have given full, constant, remunerative employment for a far larger quantity of private and public capital than is now employed.[6]

This sort of iffy history assumes much more than can be proven. If all classes had equal access to land, would there have been a large enough working class to man the factories introduced by the industrial revolution? And would capitalists have undertaken speculative investments in new industries, instead of in trade or in land, if there had not been the opportunities to make enormous profits in manufacturing? Moreover, where would the original accumulation of capital used in industry have come from if not from the extraction of wealth from colonies, piracy, and the slave trade—as described by Marx in *Capital* (Vol. I, Part VIII)? Finally, where would the reproduction and growth of the needed capital for investment have come from if not from sufficiently large profits arising in the operation of enterprise?

True, it is possible to conceive an ideal situation where production and consumption can be balanced, where "whatever is produced in England can be consumed in England." But then we have to posit a society which is subjected to rational social control instead of relying on the market servo-mechanism regulated by the need for profits. In most manufacturing industries capacity and production cannot be regulated to conform exactly to consumer demand. For example, assume that steel cannot be efficiently produced unless there is a complement of equipment that has the capacity to produce 100,000 tons. If the demand turns out to be 150,000 tons, the manufacturer has the choice of missing out on the extra market opportunity or of taking a chance and adding another 100,000 tons of capacity. If he adds the capacity, he has a surplus capacity of 50,000 tons. To get a proper return on his investment he must then seek extra markets. This is but one of the many factors which create pressure for expanding markets, both foreign and domestic. The entire mechanism of a market economy—competition, fluctuations in consumer demand, uneven development of complementary industries, technological changes, the accumulation of profits—force a restless drive of capital to expand.

This being the case, Hobson's panacea of an increase in consumer income is unrealistic. He assumes in effect that coordinated direction of economic change is possible by increasing wage levels. However, this device can hardly be relied upon to get the results Hobson sought. For example, too rapid a rise in consumption may under some circumstances reduce profit levels sufficiently to stall the engine of capital accumulation, resulting in insufficient employment opportunities for a labor supply swelled by population increase and those displaced by rising productivity. Alternatively, if the rise in consumption is not large enough to halt accumulation, it tends to spur further speculative bouts of capital investment and to raise the imbalance of capacity and consumption to a new level. Unfortunately, Hobson's prescription merely follows the common illusion that capital investment can be regulated not by planning, but by adjusting one of the variables in the capitalist economic process. What he ignores is that such manipulation, even if feasible, sets off a series of new dislocations.

For the sake of protecting profits and capital investment, the avid exploration of sales-opportunities in the world markets must accompany the inexorable expansion of capacity. And, as Hobson explains, the structure of industry itself becomes adapted to the world market rather than to the domestic market alone. On the other hand, Hobson does not take account of the way this development is involved with changes in the rest of a business society's international life—with, for example, international banking, the international money market, and the constraints of the balance of payments.

Given the kind of industrial and financial structure that evolves over time, and the organization of class power that operates this structure, the idealistic constructs of Hobson are not available as realistic options for even reform governments. Witness, for example, how the British Labour Party, despite its avowed socialist ideology, has behaved on matters of empire and international economic arrangements whenever it has come to power. Even though it eventually presided over the dissolution of the formal British Empire—not by choice, but by necessity—it realistically managed the dissolution so that there would be as smooth a transition as possible to an informal empire that would serve the same imperialist economic policies.

A similar lesson can be learned from the experience of Roosevelt's New Deal. The New Deal's important social reforms and energetic pump-priming did not succeed in accelerating the capital accumulation engine; only the ample profits of foreign war orders and domestic military business provided the impetus. The foreign operations of the New Deal were similarly realistic in terms of the options available in the then existing economic and social situation, adding up to a drive to gain foreign markets and special advantages in these markets for U.S. business. (The details on this argument are well analyzed in the book by Lloyd C. Gardner, *Economic Aspects of New Deal Diplomacy*, Madison, Wisconsin, 1964.)

Realism is also the hallmark of a more recent public program introduced under a liberal and progressive banner. J. J. Servan-Schreiber in his very popular book, *The American Challenge*, explores the danger of Western Europe becoming a satellite of the U.S. economy, as a result of the spread of American capital throughout Western Europe. Servan-Schreiber's avowed aims are to avoid the colonization of the area and, at the same time, to encourage ideals of social justice and individual dignity. He is, however, a man of realism and accepts the existing social system as a necessary condition. Once he bases his reasoning on the continuation of capitalism, Servan-Schreiber's prescription is obvious and logical: Western Europe must develop the right kind of muscle to be able to compete with U.S. business; the 50 to 100 largest European companies must be given the opportunity and encouragement to merge so that they will be large enough to take on the U.S. giants; hence, Western European countries must federate and provide the research funds and enough government business to give the enlarged industrial giants a leg up for better competitive strength. Thus, the path to independence for Western Europe, to social justice, and to social progress is: Big Government and Big Business for economic war with the United States moloch.

Students frequently put the question: Is imperialism necessary? The point I am trying to make here and in the analysis presented in the following chapters is that such a question is off the mark. Imperialism is not a matter of choice for a capitalist society; it is the way of life of such a society.

NOTES

1. Not that minor economic influences should be ignored. Marginal economic forces can at times carry extra special weight—as one can easily learn, for example, from Robert Engler's *The Politics of Oil* (New York, 1967). Economic effects which are marginal to the economy as a whole may be of major importance to certain giant corporations. Accordingly, they can be inordinately influential on public policy because of the concentration of economic and political power in the hands of these corporations.
2. David S. Landes, "The Nature of Economic Imperialism" in *The Journal of Economic History*, December 1961, p. 510.
3. Mark Blaug, "Economic Imperialism Revisited," *The Yale Review*, Spring 1961, p. 343.
4. Barbara Ward, *The West at Bay*, New York, 1948, p. 136.
5. See, for example, William Appleman Williams, *The Tragedy of American Diplomacy*, New York, 1962.
6. J. A. Hobson, *Imperialism—A Study*, 1902 (Paperback edition: Ann Arbor, Michigan, 1965, pp. 88-89). Whatever criticisms may be made of it, Hobson's work on imperialism marked an historic turning point in the study of the subject. Both Hilferding (*Das Finanzkapital*, 1910) and Lenin (*Imperialism, The Highest Stage of Capitalism*, 1917) were directly and deeply influenced by Hobson.

2

THE NEW IMPERIALISM

A focal point of Lenin's theory of imperialism is the classification of imperialism as a special stage in the development of capitalism, arising towards the end of the 19th century. This attempt to give imperialism such a specific historical reference date has been a subject of controversy, the main objection being that many of the features considered characteristic of imperialism are found early in the game and throughout the history of capitalism: the urgency to develop a world market, the struggle to control foreign sources of raw materials, the competitive hunt for colonies, and the tendency towards concentration of capital.

Some scholars get around this problem by distinguishing between an "old" and a "new" imperialism. Whatever semantic device is used, there are good and sufficient reasons for clearly marking off a new period in the affairs of world capitalism. Of the many distinguishing features of this new stage, two, in my opinion, are decisive: First, England is no longer the undisputed leading industrial power. Strong industrialized rivals appear on the scene: the United States, Germany, France, and Japan. Second, within each of the industrialized nations, economic power shifts to a relatively small number of big integrated industrial and financial firms.

The framework for these developments was provided by the introduction during the last 20 to 30 years of the 19th century of new sources of energy and a new departure in technology, which Veblen called "the technology of physics and chemistry."

This is a technology that is based on the direct application of science and scientific research, rather than on mere mechanical ingenuity. It was in the final 30 years of the 19th century that:

. . . a whole century of slow progress and restatement in pure science—particularly in thermodynamics, electromagnetism, chemistry and geology—began to meet up with rapid development in practical mechanical engineering—and particularly in the production of machine-tools—and in industrial methods . . . not only were new industries developed and new sources of power provided— the internal combustion engine, stemming from progress in thermodynamics theory, being only less important than electricity. Innumerable existing industries—mining and road-building, steel, agriculture, petroleum, concrete are but a few examples—were transformed and expanded. Innumerable new products—the modern bicycle, the telephone, the typewriter, linoleum, the pneumatic tyre, cheap paper, artificial silk, aluminum, ready-made clothing and shoes—were manufactured and marketed for the first time. It was in this period that mechanization first became characteristic of industry in general. . . .[1]

Even more important than the technological features of this period per se is that this technology as a rule required investment of large amounts of capital and large production units. The main developments that characterize the transformation occurred in steel, electricity, industrial chemistry, and oil.[2]

Steel. Steel has unique properties that are essential in the construction of machines such as internal combustion engines, electric generators, and steam turbines. It was the introduction of steel rails and locomotives that made possible the carrying of heavy loads at high speeds. This reduced the cost of transport and provided the means for transforming local and regional businesses into large, national industries.

Before the application of scientific methods, steel was practically a semi-precious metal. "Until [Bessemer and open-hearth] processes were introduced steel making was hardly more than an empirical craft operation. . . ."[3] The Bessemer process, introduced in 1854, still had limitations for the use of iron ore available in the United States and Europe. The open-hearth method introduced in the 1860's, and finally the "basic process" developed by Thomas and Gilchrist in 1875 made possible the control of the carbon content of steel within very close limits—and opened up the age of steel. Techniques for improving the properties of steel by use of alloys—to obtain the qualities needed for tool steel, armaments, and stainless steel—were developed between 1870 and 1913. Note that during the period 1870-1874 an average of 1 million tons of steel were produced worldwide; during 1900-1904, the annual average world production had risen to over 27 million tons.[4]

Electricity. While scientific experiments with electricity and theoretical exploration of the subject go back to the 18th century, the application of these experiments and theory to form a large-scale industry occurs toward the end of the 19th century. The first commercial generating stations in London, Milan, and New York were opened in the 1880's. The importance of electricity is not limited to its use as a new source of light, heat, and power. It is necessary, for example, in the refinement of copper and aluminum and the bulk production of caustic soda. (The invention of the process for commercial production of aluminum also stems from this period, occurring in 1886.) For manufacturing processes in general, the application of electricity made possible the kind of precise control which permitted the more complete mechanization on which modern mass-production industry depends.

Industrial Chemistry. Chemical processes in metallurgy, tanning, and fermentation had been known and used for many centuries. But industrial chemistry as a separate and large-scale industry originates in the last third of the 19th century. Here again the transformation is due to theoretical and experimental discoveries in science. The ability to synthesize organic chemicals in industrial processes could not appear before the proper understanding of chemical transformations was achieved. Thus the ability to determine the correct number of atoms in a molecule became possible once there was general recognition around 1860 of the law that equal volumes of gases under the same conditions contain the same number of molecules. The effective concept of the structural arrangement of atoms in a molecule comes in 1865. In contrast with the former almost accidental advances in organic chemistry, the new scientific achievements created the basis for new mass-production industries. The Solvay ammonia soda process and the catalytic processes for the manufacture of sulphuric acid and of ammonia belong also to the same period.

Oil. Here we are not dealing so much with technical and scientific advances as with the discovery and exploration of underground petroleum sources, though of course technical and scientific achievements are significant both in the techniques of extracting crude oil and in petroleum refining. From the historical point of view, it should be noted that large quantities of oil were first discovered in Pennsylvania in 1859. The Standard Oil Company was founded in 1870. Diamond drilling, the effective technique for piercing hard formations, was first invented in 1864 and was introduced in the United States in the 1870's.

The earliest phase of large oil discoveries was concerned with nationwide and international distribution systems for oil in kerosene lamps and for the manufacture of lubricants. The introduction of oil as fuel in industry and transportation follows from later discoveries of oil sources.

Sometimes referred to as a "second industrial revolution," these new phenomena were integral to the shift from a capitalism characterized by dispersed small competitive units to one in which large concentrations of economic power dominated the industrial and financial scene. How significant these late 19th century technological developments were in accelerating monopolistic trends can be seen by examining the giant corporations of today:

- Of the 50 largest industrial corporations in the United States today, 26 (accounting for 62 percent of the total assets of the whole group) are in steel, oil, electrical equipment, chemicals, and aluminum.

- Of the 50 largest industrial corporations in capitalist countries outside the United States, 30 (accounting for 73 percent of the total assets of the group) are in these same industries.

The Rise of Big Business

Our argument here is not that the new technology determined the size of the corporation and the monopolistic trends that accompanied Big Business. Rather, the new technology provided the framework, and often the opportunity, for the quite normal tendencies of capitalist industry toward concentration of power. For example, the transcontinental railroad and its feeders created the possibility for local manufacturers to compete on a national scale. The overexpansion of production that resulted from many local producers' expanding their capacity to meet the enlarged markets resulted in ruthless competition, failures, mergers, and alliances—a familiar pattern of business history. The transformation that took place in the United States business life during the onset of the imperialist stage is well summarized by Professor Chandler:

In the 1870's, the major industries serviced an agrarian economy. Except for a few companies equipping the rapidly expanding railroad network, the leading industrial firms processed agricultural products and provided farms with food and clothing. These firms tended to be small, and bought their raw materials and sold their finished goods locally. Where they manufactured for a market more than a few miles away from the factory, they bought and sold through commissioned agents who handled the business of several other similar firms.

By the beginning of the twentieth century, many more companies were making producers' goods, to be used in industry, rather than on the farm or by the ultimate consumer. Most of the major industries had become dominated by a few large enterprises. These great industrial corporations no longer purchased and sold through agents, but they had their own nation-wide buying and marketing organizations. Many, primarily those in the extractive industries, had come to control their own raw materials. In other words, the business economy had become industrial. *Major industries were dominated by a few firms that had become great, vertically integrated, centralized enterprises.* (Emphasis added.)[5]

The Civil War and the railroad expansion provided the opportunity for the maturation of powerful financial institutions that could accumulate the capital and organize the mergers that became what Chandler identifies as the "great, vertically integrated, centralized enterprises."[6] The new technological innovations discussed above provided the material production

bases for such Big Business. The frequent depressions that began in 1873 were the battleground. And the method of business
organization for this transformation was the corporation—what
Veblen termed the "master institution of civilized life."

The New Drive for Raw Materials

The new industries, the new technology and the rise of
competition among industrialized nations gave a new importance
to the role of raw materials. The struggle for the control of iron
ore and coking coal on the European continent is a familiar
story. Even more important was the pressure to gain control
over distant territories whose value assumed new relevance.
Barraclough summarizes this trend as follows:

. . . the voracious appetite of the new industrialism, unable of
its very nature to draw sufficient sustenance from local resources,
rapidly swallowed up the whole world. It was no longer a question
of exchanging European manufactures—predominantly textiles—
for traditional oriental and tropical products, or even of providing
outlets for the expanding iron and steel industries by building railways, bridges and the like. *Industry now went out into the world
in search of the basic materials without which, in its new forms, it
could not exist.* (Emphasis added.)[7]

This was part of a general new pattern of economic relations in the world capitalist system. During the period from
1860 to 1900, three changes in the economic relations between
nations are notable: (1) the number of commodities entering
international trade on a large scale multiplied greatly; (2)
competition between many widely separated regions of the world
first appeared or grew more intense; and (3) the standard
of living of workers and the profitability of industry in European
nations came to depend on maintenance of overseas supplies,
while the standard of living of the producers of raw materials
came to depend on market fluctuations occurring sometimes on
the other side of the world.[8]

As the need for raw materials grew, the rate of discovery
and exploitation of the resources increased. "It was the same
thirty years [from 1870 to 1900] that most of the undeveloped
agricultural areas of the world were opened up and that, with
the increase of geological knowledge, though not all were yet

exploited, most of the world's great mineral-bearing districts were discovered."[9] It was in the last quarter of the 19th century that nickel was discovered and developed in Canada, copper and zinc in Australia, nitrogen in Chile, and tin and rubber in Malaya. In sum:

> The ring of distant primary producers was widened from North America, Roumania and Russia to tropical and sub-tropical lands and, beyond them, to Australasia and South Africa. *Areas and lines of commerce that had previously been self-contained dissolved into a single economy on a world scale.* (Emphasis added.)[10]

Advance in Ocean Transportation and the World Market

World commerce, as noted earlier, was an essential ingredient of early capitalism and it progressed as capitalism matured. But a new leap forward, involving the feasibility of moving cheaply the bulk raw materials needed for the new giant industries, was made possible by the mass production of steel and technical innovations in shipbuilding. Metal-built steamships using steel hulls, steel boilers, twin screws, and compound engines—a "synthesis of existing inventions"—became the predominant form of ocean transport in the last two decades of the 19th century.[11] The problems posed by the higher pressures needed in marine engines "were not solved till the later 1870's and early 1880's when improved steel boilers and tubes enabled shipbuilders to construct ships with triple expansion engines that worked at 150 lb. pressure and more."[12]

The demand for efficient and cheap bulk shipment of heavy products throughout the world, the new metal steamship which made it possible, and rapid communication (trans-Atlantic cable service began in 1866) set the stage for a commercial revolution. This commercial revolution was financed by the simultaneous growth of international banking and the creation of a "single multilateral system of international payments. A world market, governed by world prices, emerged for the first time."[13]

Empire and the New Imperialism

The above developments also contributed to a speed-up in the industrialization of lands other than England—the United

States, Germany, Japan, France, Belgium, and others. This industrialization occurred under circumstances in which concentration of economic power in large business units, mobilization of large masses of capital for particular projects, growth of protective tariffs, and a wave of militarization[14] provided the framework for what was essentially new in the imperialism of the late 19th and 20th centuries. Above all, what was new was the extension of imperialist behavior patterns to most industrialized nations.[15] It was no longer Britain controlling international commerce, carving out spheres of commercial influence, and picking up a colony here and there. Instead, it was the economic and political operations of other rapidly advancing countries rushing for their place in the sun which pinned a new label on modern society.

Under the impetus of this new imperialism no corner of the earth was left untouched: the entire world was transformed and adapted to the needs of the new dominant industry in each industrialized nation, and to the rivalry between these nations under the pressure of these needs.

Imperialism and Colonies

The complex of economic and political relations that arose from or were an accommodation to these specially new phenomena encompasses the imperialist era. The change thus marked off is not an abrupt one: it flows directly from well-entrenched tendencies inherent in a capitalist economy. The principal new feature is the concentration of economic power in giant corporations and financial institutions, with the consequent internationalization of capital.

The urge to dominate is integral to business. Risks abound in the business world. Internal and external competition, rapid technological changes, depressions, to name but a few, threaten not only the rate of profit but the capital investment itself. Business therefore is always on the lookout for ways of controlling its environment—to eliminate as much risk as possible. In industry after industry, the battle for survival has also been a battle for conquest, from which the giant corporations best fitted for their environment have emerged. Their

ways and habits are the result of a process of adaptation to the
battle for survival and growth; these ways and habits have been
built into their organizational structures and their modes of
operation as ways of guaranteeing and sustaining victory.

(1) The most obvious first requirement to assure safety
and control in a world of tough antagonists is to gain control
over as much of the sources of raw materials as possible—
*wherever these raw materials may be, including potential new
sources.*[16]

Controlling raw materials sources is both a protective
device against pressure of competitors as well as a weapon of
offense to keep non-integrated competitors in line. Ownership
of and control over raw material supplies is, as a rule, an essential prerequisite for the ability of a leading firm or group
of leading firms to limit new competition and to control production and prices of the finished products. Moreover, the very
size of the large vertically integrated firms gives them the
resources to explore and develop potential new supplies throughout the world.[17] The history of the oil industry is of course a
classic illustration, but this principle applies also to the aluminum,
steel, copper, and other industries.

(2) The pattern of most successful manufacturing businesses includes conquest of foreign markets. This is so even
where there is as large an internal market as in the United
States. In the mass market auto industry, for example, foreign
markets exercised an important influence from the earliest days.
The sixth Ford car built was shipped to a Canadian distributor.
The Ford Motor Company in its first year of operation started
making arrangements for building up its foreign markets.[18]

Despite the very high rate of domestic population increase
and the opportunities available in the underdeveloped regions
of this country, the drive to develop exports of manufactures
took root during the very first flush of industrial maturity—
less than a decade after the end of the Civil War. In 1871 little
over 7 percent of United States exports consisted of finished
manufactures; by 1890 this percent rose to almost 12 percent;
by 1900 to almost 19 percent.[19] The succession of depressions
from 1873 to the turn of the century produced two responses:

internally, a wave of consolidations and the move towards Big Business; externally, the drive to capture export markets, including those of industrialized Europe.[20]

The dynamics of this search for export markets varies from industry to industry, and has different degrees of importance at various stages in the evolution of an industry and in different phases of the business cycle. What must be understood in any case is the special significance for industry to maintain these export markets. Lenin's generalization on this point is most appropriate: "The growth of internal exchange, and particularly of international exchange, is the characteristic distinguishing feature of capitalism. The uneven and spasmodic character of the development of individual enterprises, of individual branches of industry and individual countries, is inevitable under the capitalist system."[21]

Foreign markets are pursued (with the aid and support of the state) to provide the growth rate needed to sustain a large investment of capital and to exploit new market opportunities. In this process, the dependence on export markets becomes a permanent feature, for these markets coalesce with the structure of industrial capacity. In one period exports may be the only way out of disaster; in another they may be the best way to maintain the flow of profits. But as the filling of foreign orders becomes built into the capacity and overhead of the business firm, the pressure to maintain these foreign markets over the long run becomes ever more insistent—especially as competitors arrive on the scene.[22]

(3) Foreign investment is an especially effective method for the development and protection of foreign markets. The clearest historic demonstration of this was the export of capital for railways, which stimulated at the same time the demand for rails, locomotives, railway cars, and other products of the iron, steel, and machine industries.[23]

But this method of penetrating foreign markets becomes ever more prevalent in the age of the giant corporation, characterized as it is by intensification of national rivalries. The role of foreign investment to capture and exploit sources of raw materials is evident. More than this, though, is the urgency of foreign investment to withstand the competition, or to pre-empt markets, in the countries where competitive corporate giants also exist.

The foreign corporate giants can swing their own weight in controlling their own domestic markets, or in their preferential markets—such as in colonies, dependencies, or "spheres of influence." They can also use their political strength to set up protective tariffs and other trade barriers against outsiders. For these reasons, the ability to compete in other countries and to exercise the kind of market control needed by the giant corporations calls for a program of foreign investment. The competition between corporate giants resolves itself either in cartel arrangements or in permanent invasion of each others' markets via the route of foreign investment. Moreover, this procedure becomes more feasible in the age of Big Business, thanks to the large masses of capital available to large corporations from their own profits or from what they can mobilize in cooperation with financial institutions.

The foregoing reasons for the spurt of foreign investment in the age of imperialism are far from exhaustive. There is naturally the attractiveness of increasing profit rates through taking advantage of lower labor costs abroad. Observe, for example, how The Chase Manhattan Bank slips in information on wage rates in South Korea in its report spelling out the attractiveness of investing in that country.

In fact, the main impetus for Korea's economic growth comes from the determination and drive of its businessmen and officials. Americans comment on the dexterity and aptitude of Korean workers, who are available at cash wage rates averaging 65¢ a day in textiles and 88¢ a day in electronics. These human characteristics produce industrial results.[24]

Attractive as lower costs are, their appeal is not necessarily the main attraction of foreign investment. It is merely one of the influences. Much more important is the spur of developing raw material resources, creating demand for exports, and taking advantage of "monopoly" situations. The latter arises due to cost advantages of Big Business, exclusive patents, superior technology, or preferred market demand stimulated by establishment of desired brands via sales promotion. Finally, foreign investment arises from the pressure to establish trade in markets protected by tariff walls or trade preferences. (United States investment in Canada, for example, is a convenient arrangement for participating in British Empire trade.)

The commonly held notion that the theory of imperialism should be concerned largely with investment in underdeveloped countries just isn't correct. The fact is that profitable investment opportunities in such countries are limited by the very conditions imposed by the operations of imperialism. Restricted market demand and industrial backwardness are products of the lopsided economic and social structures associated with the transformation of these countries into suppliers of raw materials and food for the metropolitan centers.

Our purpose here is not to analyze exhaustively all the factors involved in foreign investment. Rather, it is to suggest that there are clear reasons for the spurt of foreign investment in the age of imperialism—as a consequence of the opportunities and pressures accompanying the rise of Big Business. This is not prompted by the malice of the businessman, but by the normal and proper functioning of business in the conditions confronted. The patterns of these investments should be examined in their historical context, in light of the actual situations business firms deal with, rather than in the more usual terms of an abstraction concerning the pressure of surplus capital.[25]

(4) The drive for foreign investment opportunities and control over foreign markets brings the level of political activity on economic matters to a new and intense level. The last quarter of the 19th century sees the spread of protective tariffs.[26] Other political means—threats, wars, colonial occupation—are valuable assistants in clearing the way to exercise sufficient political influence in a foreign country to obtain privileged trade positions, to get ownership of mineral rights, to remove obstacles to foreign trade and investment, to open the doors to foreign banks and other financial institutions which facilitate economic entry and occupation.

The degree and type of political operation naturally vary. In weak outlying territories, colonial occupation is convenient. In somewhat different circumstances, bribery of officials or loans (via banks or state institutions) are appropriate.[27] Among the more advanced countries, alliances and interest groups are formed.

The result of these developments is a new network of international economic and political relations. The network itself changes in shape and emphasis over time as a result of wars, depressions, and differential rates of industrialization.[28] The forms also vary: colonies, semi-colonies, "a variety of forms of dependent countries—countries, which, officially, are politically independent, but which are in fact, enmeshed in the net of financial and diplomatic dependence,"[29] and junior and senior partners among the imperialist powers. The significant theme is the different degrees of dependence in an international economy, an international economy in continuous ferment as a result of the battles among giant corporations over the world scene and the operations of these corporations along with their state governments to maintain domination and control over weaker nations.

The oversimplification which identifies imperialism with colonialism pure and simple neither resembles Lenin's theory nor the facts of the case. Similarly fallacious is the version of Lenin's theory that imperialism is in essence the need of advanced countries to get rid of a surplus which chokes them, and that this surplus is divested through productive investments in colonies.

The stage of imperialism, as we have tried to show, is much more complex than can be explained by any simple formula. The drive for colonies is not only economic but involves as well political and military considerations in a world of competing imperialist powers. Likewise, the pressures behind foreign investment are more numerous and more involved than merely exporting capital to backward countries. There is no simple explanation for all the variations of real economic and political changes, nor is it fruitful to seek one. The special value of Lenin's theory is the highlighting of all the principal levers that have moved international economic relations. These levers are the ones associated with the new stage of monopoly and the essential ways monopoly operates to achieve, wherever and whenever feasible, domination and control over sources of supply and over markets. The fact that these are still the principal levers explains why the theory is still relevant. But the particular forms in which these factors operate and become adapted to new conditions requires continuous re-examination.

Modern Features of Imperialism

The imperialism of today has several distinctly new features. These are, in our opinion: (1) the shift of the main emphasis from rivalry in carving up the world to the struggle against the contraction of the imperialist system; (2) the new role of the United States as organizer and leader of the world imperialist system; and (3) the rise of a technology which is international in character.

(1) The Russian Revolution marks the beginning of the new phase. Before the Second World War the main features were the expansion of imperialism to cover the globe, and the conflicts among the powers for the redistribution of territory and spheres of influence. After the Russian Revolution, a new element was introduced into the competitive struggle: the urge to reconquer that part of the world which had opted out of the imperialist system and the need to prevent others from leaving the imperialist network. With the end of the Second World War, the expansion of the socialist part of the world and the break-up of most of the colonial system intensified the urgency of saving as much as possible of the imperialist network and reconquering the lost territories. Conquest in this context takes on different forms, depending on the circumstances: military and political as well as economic.

While the imperialist powers did not give up the colonies gladly or easily, the main purposes of colonialism had been achieved prior to the new political independence: the colonies had been intertwined with the world capitalist markets; their resources, economies, and societies had become adapted to the needs of the metropolitan centers. The current task of imperialism now became to hold on to as many of the economic and financial benefits of these former colonies as possible. And this of course meant continuation of the economic and financial dependency of these countries on the metropolitan centers.

Neither in the period right after the Russian Revolution nor in our own day does the central objective of extending and/or defending the frontiers of imperialism signify the elimination of rivalries among the imperialist powers. However, since the end of the Second World War this central objective has dominated the scene because of the increasing threat to the imperialist system and because of the greater unity among the powers imposed by United States leadership.[30]

(2) Up to the end of the Second World War political and military operations in the imperialist world system were carried on in the traditional method of alignment in blocs: competitive interests in one bloc were temporarily repressed for the sake of a joint offense or defense against another bloc. The composition of these blocs changed over time as did the tactical advantages sought. Since 1945 the new phenomenon is the assumption by the United States of leadership of the entire imperialist system. As a result of its maturing economic and military strength and the destruction inflicted on rivals by the war, the United States had the capacity and the opportunity to organize and lead the imperialist network of our time.

The organizing of the postwar imperialist system proceeded through the medium of the international agencies established toward the end of the war: the United Nations, the World Bank, and the International Monetary Fund—in each of which the United States was able, for various reasons, to exercise the leading role. The system was consolidated through the activities of UNRRA, the Marshall Plan, and the several economic and military aid programs financed and controlled from Washington.

The new perspective of United States leadership was referred 'to indirectly by Secretary of State Rusk when he called attention to the fact that the United States is "criticized not for sacrificing our national interests to international interests but for endeavoring to *impose the international interest upon other nations.*" (Emphasis added.) This criticism is not rejected by the Secretary of State. Indeed, he is proud of it: "This criticism is, I think, a sign of strength—of our strength and the strength of international law." Further, he continues to spell out the ambitious vista of United States foreign policy:

> But we know we can no longer find security and well-being in defenses and policies which are confined to North America, or the Western Hemisphere, or the North Atlantic community.
> This has become a very small planet. We have to be concerned with all of it—with all of its land, waters, atmosphere, and with surrounding space.[31]

In view of the limitations of the United Nations, stemming from participation of socialist countries, the practical administration of this global and spatial concern was affected by a series of treaties and declarations covering the non-socialist world. A list of these instruments as of August, 1966 is given in Appendix A (pp.203-206).

The diplomatic arrangements shown in this list were stimulated and given substance by the proliferation of military bases around the planet. The new role of the United States in this respect can be seen in the fact that U.S. armed forces in the 1920's were stationed in only three countries abroad. During the Second World War, U.S. armed forces were to be found in 39 countries. Today, through distribution of military assistance and the direction of military training of foreign armies, U.S. military groups are located in at least 64 countries. These, as can be seen in Table I, are well spread out over the globe.

That these forces and their equipment have not remained

TABLE I

	Number of Countries in which U.S. Armed Forces are Represented
Latin America	19
East Asia (including Australia)	10
Africa	11
Europe	13
Near East and South Asia	11
	64

Source: From data in Agency for International Development, *U.S. Overseas Loans and Grants, Obligations and Loan Authorizations, July 1, 1945 to June 30, 1967,* Washington, D.C., March 29, 1968.

idle and that their presence exerts influence, even in the absence of direct action, is too obvious to need spelling out. However, just for the record, a list of United States direct military involvements since 1961 alone, as reported by the Department of State, is given in Appendix B (p. 207).

An important aspect of the new United States leadership position is its direct replacement of other imperialist powers. Eugene V. Rostow, Under Secretary of State for Political Affairs, put it this way in a radio interview: ". . . in many ways the whole postwar history has been a process of American movement to take over positions . . . of security which Britain, France, the Netherlands and Belgium had previously held."[32]

Nor has United States business been caught napping while all this has been going on. For example, United States banks abroad are no longer concentrated mainly in Latin America, but are now spread out over the globe. And the United States position in the lush Middle East oil industry has been transformed. Table II presents estimates of the change in the relative position of the United States with respect to Middle East oil. While

TABLE II
OIL RESERVES IN MIDDLE EAST
Estimates of Reserves Controlled
(The amounts are in billions of barrels)

	1940 Amount	1940 % of Total	1967 Amount	1967 % of Total
Great Britain	4.3	72.0	73.0	29.3
United States	0.6	9.8	146.0	58.6
Other	1.1	18.2	30.0	12.1
Total	6.0	100.0	249.00	100.0

Source: 1940. Based on data from Zuhayr Mikdashi, *A Financial Analysis of Middle Eastern Oil Concessions,* New York, Praeger, 1966.

1967. Based on data from *Oil and Gas Journal,* December 25, 1967. These data are estimates, based on the assumption that all the oil reserves in a country are owned by major concessionaires. If anything, this assumption results in an underestimation of the U.S. share in 1967 as compared with Great Britain.

United States firms controlled less than 10 percent of the reserves in Middle Eastern oil leases before the Second World War and 72 percent was held by Great Britain, the positions are now reversed: the United States now controls almost 59 percent while the British share has fallen to a little more than 29 percent. The reasons for this reversal are not to be sought in the greater ingenuity or ability of the United States oil industry but rather in the politics of the Middle East, the uses of United States Lend Lease during the Second World War, postwar foreign aid programs, and the ingenuity of the State Department and other government agencies.[33]

(3) The new technology, spurred on by the war, is much more international in scope than the older technology, and therefore has special implications for the current and future operation of imperialism. The most obvious aspect is the technology of space. The large number of "space" stations around the globe manned by United States technicians is one of the international features. Another is the pre-eminent role of the United States in communications satellites, so that not only *Life, Readers' Digest, Time,* Hollywood movies, and the publications of the United States Information Agency are on hand, but United States television fare is instantly available: all useful means for attaining a "cultural" unity which mirrors the United States guidance of the imperialist system. With this have also come new international legal arrangements, as noted by Secretary Rusk: "And to start building a single global communications satellite system, we have created a novel international institution in which a private American corporation shares ownership with 45 governments."[34]

In addition, the technologies of atomic energy and computers have special international features. The enormous investment in research and development required for these industries gives a special edge to the corporations which are large enough to be multinational in scale. Without trying to trace the causal interconnections, we should be aware of the happy blending of the new technology and the international corporation: (a) The United States has firms which are large enough to have, or be able to obtain, sufficient capital to develop the necessary technology and take advantage of pre-empting the field in other countries. (b) United States firms are supported in this technical lead by huge government grants of research and development. (c) These same firms have had experience in international operations, either on their own or in cooperation with the United States government in the process of the latter's stretching its various military and foreign aid activities around the globe. (d) Along with generous government assistance has come an integrated apparatus of scientific research and technical development in the large corporation, one result of which is the considerable reduction of the lead time between scientific advances and the introduction of new products, thus giving the international corporation a global edge over smaller and less powerful rivals. Finally, (e) the technological advances embodied in the jet plane have made more feasible the coordinated management of the multinational corporation.

Demand for External Sources of Raw Materials

One of the features of imperialism that persists unabated to this day is the reliance of the giant corporation for its monopolistic position, including the size of its profits, on foreign sources of raw materials. What is new in today's imperialism is that the United States has become a "have-not" nation for a wide range of both common and rare minerals.

A strange sort of reasoning crops up these days in academic discussions of this subject because advanced industrialized countries are importing a smaller value of raw materials in proportion to output of final products than in the past. This trend reflects increasing efficiency in the industrial uses of raw materials resulting from: (1) improvements in technology and design; (2) increased complexity of consumer products (that is, more manufacturing work is applied to a given amount of raw materials); (3) development of synthetic materials (rubber, plastics, fibers); and (4) improved organization of scrap collection and utilization.

This increasing efficiency in raw materials use is undoubtedly important. It has a serious bearing on the prosperity and viability of the underdeveloped primary commodity producing countries. It is an important contributor to the differential rates of growth between the industrialized and non-industrialized countries. It is involved in the increasing financial dependency of many underdeveloped economies, which will be discussed below. But a strange leap in reasoning is needed to conclude that the strategic role of raw materials has changed for the advanced countries. No matter how efficient industry becomes in the use of aluminum or in the extraction of alumina from bauxite, you can't make aluminum without bauxite and you can't make an airplane without aluminum. And when in the United States, 80 to 90 percent of the bauxite supply comes from foreign sources, the assurance of such supply is of crucial importance to the aluminum industry, the airplane industry, and the country's military power.

Another factor often cited as tending to minimize the raw materials problem is the technical achievements in the processing of low-grade ores, and the use of substitute materials (e.g. plastics for metals). Significant technical strides have indeed been made but, as the data we are about to present will show, these achievements have not reversed the trend. With all the amazing accomplishments of scientists and the wonders of electronics and atomic energy, they still have not discovered how to make ordinary metals behave, except within narrow limits, according to the will of the user.

What may seem dramatic in the laboratory or in a pilot plant is often a far cry from what is needed in practice to transform an entire industry. Managers of business may plan for the future, but they live in the present. Any president of a big corporation who did not aggressively pursue acquisition of foreign leases for raw materials because in the historical long run a domestic substitute will probably be found, would most properly be fired from his job.

Thinking in terms of national planning (for the good of the people) or in abstract economic analysis (in terms of cost curves) does not help to understand the impact of foreign raw materials supplies on the policies of business and government. The question boils down to the nature of control and behavior in business, and the government's realistic response to the operational needs of business. Thus, great developments in the exploitation and use of shale oil, which may some day eliminate domestic dependency on foreign sources, do not and will not diminish the rivalry among oil firms to acquire every bit of oil under land or sea they can lay their hands on. The decisive issues are not consumer and social needs but the controls business firms desire in order to manage world production and prices for the sake of greater profits.

While monopolistic behavior patterns produce the eager drive for foreign supply sources, the shift of the United States from a "have" to a "have-not" nation has likewise resulted in an intensification of the urgency to obtain and control foreign resources. The central point for minerals industries is shown in Table III. As can be seen from the last column of this table,

TABLE III
MINERALS: NET IMPORTS COMPARED WITH CONSUMPTION*
— Annual Averages in Millions of 1954 Dollars —

Period	Imports	Exports	Net Imports**	Apparent Domestic Consumption	Net Imports As Percent of Consumption**
1900-1909	$ 323	$ 374	$ —51	$ 3,313	—1.5%
1910-1919	534	694	—160	5,135	—3.1
1920-1929	915	863	52	7,025	0.7
1930-1939	792	749	43	6,812	0.6
1940-1944	1,494	922	572	10,802	5.3
1945-1949	1,653	990	663	12,064	5.5
1950-1959	3,103	1,026	2,077	16,170	12.8
1961	3,647	1,145	2,502	17,894	14.0

* All minerals except gold.
** A minus sign means that exports were larger than imports.
Source: U.S. Bureau of the Census. Working Paper No. 6, "Raw Materials in the United States Economy: 1900-1961" (Washington, D.C., 1963.)

up until the 1920's, the United States was a net exporter of minerals; the change in trend is postponed by the depression when consumption of raw material declined. The situation, however, reverses significantly during the war years. But the new situation faced by the United States, simultaneous with its new role as organizer and leader of the imperialist network, shows up dramatically in the 1950's, when in place of its former position as a net exporter, close to 13 percent of domestic consumption is supplied by imports.

This change did not occur because of the growing need to import esoteric materials not found in the United States. On the contrary, the reason was the rapid jump in imports of the more common materials which traditionally were abundant in this country. This can be seen in Table IV, where a comparison is made between net imports of six garden-variety minerals and the domestic extraction of these materials: the situation today is compared with the prewar years.

TABLE IV
SELECTED MINERALS: NET IMPORTS AS A PERCENT OF DOMESTIC MINE OR WELL PRODUCTION

	1937-39 Average (percentages)	1966 (percentages)
Iron Ore	3	43
Copper	—13	18
Lead	0	131
Zinc	7	140
Bauxite	113	638
Petroleum	—4	31

Net Imports equals imports minus exports.

Source: 1937-39. Calculated from data in U.S. Bureau of the Census, *Statistical Abstract of the United States*: 1939, Washington, D.C., and *ibid.*, 1940.

1966. Calculated from data in U.S. Department of Interior, *Minerals Yearbook, 1966,* Washington, D.C., 1967.

Note: These data do not deal with total consumption. The latter includes refining from scrap and use of inventories. This table only represents the change in the dependency on imports as compared with use of domestic natural resources.

Note especially the data on iron ore. Back in the years just before the war, net imports of iron ore amounted to about 3 percent of the close to 52 million tons of iron ore extracted from domestic sources. In 1966, net imports were equal to 43 percent of the 90 million tons mined in the country. (The latter includes the mining of such taconite as we have learned and choose to use productively.) The exhaustion of high-quality domestic ore supplies occasioned a dramatic rise in foreign investment to develop more efficient and richer sources of iron ore in Canada, Venezuela, Brazil, and Africa. The purpose, as it developed, was not only to exploit more profitable sources of supply but to map out greater control over this essential raw material as a preventive measure: each large domestic producer naturally anticipates similar moves by other domestic and foreign producers.

It is true that in recent years technical innovations have increased the utility of domestic ores. Nevertheless, the tendency to increasing reliance on foreign sources of supply persists, partly to get one's money's worth out of an investment already made, partly as a protective device to keep the lesser quality ore sources in reserve, and partly for immediate financial advantage where foreign ores are more economical. As specialists in the field see it, in the absence of a further breakthrough in technology that would make the very low grade iron ore, derived from taconite and similar rock, decidedly cheaper than foreign ore, the prognosis is for increased reliance of our steel industry on foreign sources of ore. Thus, it is anticipated that about half of the iron ore to be consumed in 1980 will be met by foreign sources, and that by 2000 the import ratio will reach 75 percent.[85]

The dramatic reversal in the self-sufficiency of the United States with respect to raw materials was succinctly summarized in a report by the staff of the President's Commission on Foreign Economic Policy:

This transition of the United States from a position of relative self-sufficiency to one of increasing dependence upon foreign sources of supply constitutes one of the striking economic changes of our time. The outbreak of World War II marked the major turning point of this change.

Both from the viewpoint of our long-term economic growth and the viewpoint of our national defense, the shift of the United States from the position of a net exporter of metals and minerals to that of a net importer is of overshadowing significance in shaping our foreign economic policies.

We have always been almost entirely dependent on imports for tin, nickel, and the platinum group of metals. In addition, our requirements for asbestos, chromite, graphite, manganese, mercury, mica, and tungsten have been generally covered by imports. Prior to World War II this was about the extent of our list of strategic materials, that is mineral substances of which our requirements are wholly or substantially supplied by foreign sources. At present, by contrast, *the United States is fully self-sufficient only in coal, sulfur, potash, molybdenum and magnesium.* (Emphasis added.) [36]

Strategic Materials

The Defense Department operates with a list of strategic and critical materials as a guide to the stockpiling program. These are the materials which are assumed to be critical to the war potential of this country and where supply difficulties can be anticipated. However, war products are not the only ones for which these materials are strategic. Many civilian products in today's technical environment rely on the same materials. (Mica, for example, appears on this list. Mica is used in the electrical industry in condensers, telephones, dynamos, and in electric toasters.) The import dependency of these materials is shown in Table V. For more than half of these items, 80 to 100 percent of the supply in this country depends on imports.

TABLE V
CLASSIFICATION OF STRATEGIC INDUSTRIAL MATERIALS
BY DEGREE OF DEPENDENCE ON IMPORTS

Number of Materials	Ratio of Imports to New Supply (Percent)
38	80-100
6	60- 79
8	40- 59
3	20- 39
7	Less than 20
—	
62	

Source: Percy W. Bidwell, *Raw Materials,* New York, Harper & Bros., 1958, p. 12.

For 52 out of the 62 materials, at least 40 percent has to be supplied from abroad. And, according to a report of the International Development Advisory Board (a special commission set up by the President in the 1950's), *three quarters of the imported materials included in the stockpile program come from the underdeveloped areas.* The political and military response to this fact is clearly formulated by the President's Board: ". . . it is to these countries that we must look for the bulk of any possible increase in these supplies. The loss of any of these materials, through aggression, would be the equivalent of a grave military set-back."[37]

The jet engine, the gas turbine, and nuclear reactors are having an important influence on demand for materials which can only be obtained from abroad. The nature of this new need was spelled out in the report of the President's Material Policy Commission:

The advent of the gas turbine and jets for fighter aircraft, and the possible development for commercial flying and later for automobiles, has accentuated the need for materials to withstand high temperature and stress. One reason why it has taken so long to develop the gas turbine commercially is that there were no materials that could withstand red heat and at the same time take the stress of the centrifugal forces generated by 20,000 revolutions per minute. Since in the gas turbine the higher the temperature, the greater the efficiency, there is urgent need for metals, ceramics, or other substances that can operate under stress in the range above 2,000 degrees Fahrenheit.

There are also requirements for materials for carrying out nuclear reactions, many of which occur at high temperatures. Some of these materials must have a low capacity for neutron absorption as well. Thus, the need for higher and ever higher temperature resistance becomes one of our most critical problems.[38]

What this means can be seen quite clearly when we narrow our focus on one product—the jet engine, which since this report was prepared has become a commercial as well as military means of transportation. Table VI lists the six critical materials which are needed to make a jet engine. Except for molybdenum, we are dependent on imports for an adequate supply of all these items. For three of the materials, the dependence is complete. In the last column are listed the current main producers of each product in the non-Communist world. In parentheses after each country is given the percentage its output represents of total production in the non-Communist world.

TABLE VI

CRITICAL MATERIALS USED FOR JET ENGINE

	Pounds Used in Jet Engine[1]	Imports as % of Consumption[2]	Where this Material is Produced[3]
Tungsten	80-100	24%	U.S. (30%) South Korea (19%) Canada (12%) Australia (8%) Bolivia (8%) Portugal (7%)
Columbium	10-12	100%	Brazil (54%) Canada (21%) Mozambique (18%)
Nickel	1,300-1,600	75%	Canada (71%) New Caledonia (20%)
Chromium	2,500-2,800	100%	South Africa (31%) Turkey (19%) South Rhodesia (19%) Philippines (18%) Iran (5%)
Molybdenum	90-100	0	U.S. (79%) Canada (10%) Chile (9%)
Cobalt	30-40	100%	Congo (Leopoldville) (60%) Morocco (13%) Canada (12%) Zambia (11%)

1. From Percy W. Bidwell, *Raw Materials,* New York, Harper & Bros., 1958, p. 12.
2. Calculated from data in U.S. Department of Interior, *Minerals Yearbook, 1966,* Washington, D.C., 1967.
3. Major producers of the material in the non-Communist world. The percentages in parenthesis represent the amount produced in the country in 1966 as a percent of total production in non-Communist countries. The source for this information is the same as 2.

The facts presented here are of course no mystery to business or to the government planners and coordinators of policy. President Truman established in 1951 the Materials Policy

Commission, cited above, to study the materials problem of the United States and its relation to other non-Communist countries. The resulting five-volume report was issued with much publicity in the midst of the Korean War. The theme of raw materials sources as an ingredient of foreign policy crops up not only with respect to direct United States requirements but also as it concerns United States responsibility as the leader of the "free world" to see to it that Western Europe's and Japan's supplies of raw materials are assured. Consider, for example, this frank statement by former President Eisenhower:

> One of Japan's greatest opportunities for increased trade lies in a free and developing Southeast Asia. . . . The great need in one country is for raw materials, in the other country for manufactured goods. The two regions complement each other markedly By strengthening of Vietnam and helping insure the safety of the South Pacific and Southeast Asia, we gradually develop the great trade potential between this region . . . and highly industrialized Japan to the benefit of both. In this way freedom in the Western Pacific will be greatly strengthened.[39]

And finally, two more citations—one from the Republican side and one from the Democratic side of policy making. The Rockefeller Brothers Fund report on foreign economic policy offers these propositions:

> Europe's economic security today depends on two indispensable factors: (1) her own intellectual and technical vitality and economic enterprise; and (2) an international structure which will enable Europe to have access to foreign markets on fair terms and adequate supplies of materials, if Europe can offer reasonable value in return for them.
>
> Nevertheless, the economic situation of the industrialized nations remains precarious. If Asia, Middle Eastern and African nationalism, exploited by the Soviet bloc, becomes a destructive force, European supplies of oil and other essential raw materials may be jeopardized.[40]

W. W. Rostow, President Johnson's closest adviser on national security affairs, seems to be well aware of the underpinning of the imperialist network as it applies to raw materials and to the special role of the United States in today's imperialism. Testifying before the Joint Congressional Committee,

Rostow explained the relations between industrialized and under-developed nations as follows:

The location, natural resources, and populations of the under-developed areas are such that, should they become effectively attached to the Communist bloc, the United States would become the second power in the world. . . . Indirectly, the evolution of the underdeveloped areas is likely to determine the fate of Western Europe and Japan and, therefore the effectiveness of those in-dustrialized regions in the free world alliance we are committed to lead. If the underdeveloped areas fall under Communist domina-tion, or if they move to fixed hostility to the West, the economic and military strength of Western Europe and Japan will be diminished, the British Commonwealth as it is now organized will disintegrate, and the Atlantic world will become, at best, an awk-ward alliance, incapable of exercising effective influence outside a limited orbit, with the balance of the world's power lost to it. In short, our military security and our way of life as well as the fate of Western Europe and Japan are at stake in the evolution of the underdeveloped areas. We evidently have a major national interest, then, in developing a free world coalition which embraces in rea-sonable harmony and unity the industrialized states of Western Europe and Japan on the one hand, the underdeveloped areas of Asia, the Middle East, and Africa, on the other.[41]

United States as the Leading Capital Exporter

Along with the political and military changes after the Second World War, when the United States assumed the role of undisputed leader of world capitalism, came the clear-cut pre-eminence of the United States as a capital exporter. While the urgent need to develop foreign raw material sources con-tributed to the momentum of capital exports after the war, the acceleration of investment in foreign manufacturing ventures added a new dimension to the internationalization of capital.

To appreciate better this new feature, let us first examine the competitive aspects of world trade in manufactures. Table VII presents estimates of the shares of five industrial nations in world export trade in manufactures. Aside from the re-markable change in Italy's fortunes during the last two decades, and the rise of Japan's trade, the most noteworthy changes over the practically 70 years covered is the juxtaposition of the United States and the United Kingdom. Britain's share of world trade in manufactures declined from 33 to 12 percent,

while that of the United States increased from 12 to 21 percent. But note also that the United States was not able to

TABLE VII
SHARE OF EXPORTS OF MANUFACTURED GOODS
(*in percentages*)

	1899	1913	1929	1937	1950	1967
United States	11.7	13.0	20.4	19.2	26.6	20.6
United Kingdom	33.2	30.2	22.4	20.9	24.6	11.9
Germany	22.4	26.6	20.5	21.8	7.0*	19.7*
France	14.4	12.1	10.9	5.8	9.6	8.5
Italy	3.6	3.3	3.7	3.5	3.6	7.0
Japan	1.5	2.3	3.9	6.9	3.4	9.9
Others	13.2	12.5	18.2	21.9	25.2	22.4
Total	100.0	100.0	100.0	100.0	100.0	100.0

* West Germany only. A comparable figure for West Germany alone, in
  1937, is estimated at 16.5%.
Source: A. Maizels, *Industrial Growth and World Trade*, Cambridge, Eng-
          land, 1963—except for the 1967 data. (Data for 1899 and 1913
          exclude the Netherlands.) 1967 data: National Institute, *Econom-
          ic Review*, February, 1968.

maintain the lead it took right after the war: between 1950
and 1967, the United States share declined from almost 27 to
almost 21 percent, about the same as its share after the First
World War.

However, isolating just these figures is deceptive. For beginning with the First World War, and at an accelerated pace
after the Second World War, a major share of the competitive
struggle for markets was taken over by building factories or buying up businesses abroad. The new situation in this respect is
presented in Table VIII. This table shows the relative position
of leading capital exporters at the time of the First World War,
at the end of the boom of the 1920's, and in 1960. During
the initial period shown on this table, the United Kingdom
was the outstanding foreign investor: half of external capital
investments were owned by British citizens. Despite the fact
that the United States was a debtor nation until after the
First World War, it had already started to get its feet wet in

this field, beginning with the onset of its participation in the imperialist way of life.

TABLE VIII
FOREIGN INVESTMENTS OF LEADING CAPITAL EXPORTING COUNTRIES

	1914	1930	1960
	— Percent of Total —		
United Kingdom	50.3	43.8	24.5
France	22.2	8.4	4.7*
Germany	17.3	2.6	1.1
Netherlands	3.1	5.5	4.2*
Sweden	.3	1.3	.9*
United States	6.3	35.3	59.1
Canada	.5	3.1	5.5
Total	100	100	100

Source: Calculated from data in William Woodruff, *Impact of Western Man*, New York, 1966, p. 150, except for the items with asterisk.
* The data for 1960 are very broad estimates, made solely to simplify the presentation on the relative change of the U.S. position.

The interwar years, and the consequent change in position to that of a creditor nation, gave the United States its opportunity and it raced ahead to the point where it was getting close to the position of the oldest and best entrenched capital exporter. By 1960, United States foreign investments accounted for almost 60 percent of the world total. (These data apply to both portfolio and direct investment. Direct investment—the ownership of branches and subsidiaries—was the most important factor in this expansion of United States investment. Hence, if the data were shown for direct investment alone, the United States share would be even larger. While all the information is not available for the post-1960 period, it seems clear that the United States share has kept on increasing in these years as well.)

Because of this huge expansion of investment in manufacturing industries abroad, the United States is able to compete in foreign markets directly rather than by exports alone. What this means can be seen from the data in Table IX for the

TABLE IX

EXPORTS AND SALES FROM FOREIGN INVESTMENTS

(Million $)

Selected Manufacturing Industries	Sales of Foreign Affiliates			Exports From U.S.		
	1957	1965	Increase	1957	1965	Increase
Paper & Allied Products	$ 881	$1,820	$ 939	$ 223	$ 389	$ 166
Chemicals	2,411	6,851	4,440	1,457	2,402	945
Rubber Products	968	1,650	682	161	167	6
Metals	1,548	3,357	1,809	1,881	1,735	—146
Non-Electrical Machinery	1,903	5,257	3,354	3,102	5,158	2,056
Electrical Machinery & Equipment	2,047	3,946	1,899	874	1,661	787
Transportation Equipment	4,228	10,760	6,532	1,784	3,196	1,412

Source: Sales of Foreign Affiliates—Survey of Current Business, November, 1966; Exports—U.S. Bureau of the Census, Statistical Abstract of the United States: 1966 and ibid.: 1965.

years 1957 and 1965, the latest year for which such information
is presently available. The first three columns show the sales
experience of United States firms abroad (branches or subsidiaries of United States corporations). The last three columns
report the amount of exports from the United States for the
same industries.

It is especially noteworthy that in all the industries, by 1965,
the sales of foreign affiliates are higher than exports from
United States based plants. More than that, the increase during
these years has been larger in the case of foreign affiliates plants
than in exports. For the industries combined, sales of foreign-
owned plants rose 140 percent, while exports from the United
States went up 55 percent.

Sales from manufacturing firms abroad assist in the penetration of foreign markets in a double way. Not only do they
obtain a share of the market in the country in which the subsidiary is located, but they enter into the foreign trade channels
of the competing powers. This can be seen by an examination
of Table X. Thus, United States plants located in Europe sell

TABLE X
MANUFACTURING SALES ABROAD BY
FOREIGN AFFILIATES OF U.S. FIRMS
(Percent of total sales abroad)

	Canada	Latin America	Europe	Other
Local Sales	81	93	77	92
Exported to U.S.	11	2	1	2
Exported to Other Countries	8	5	22	6
Total	100	100	100	100

Source: Calculated from data in *Survey of Current Business,* November,
1966.

only 77 percent of their output to the local markets in which
the plants are located. Exports to other countries account for
22 percent of the sales of these plants. Note the relatively small
percentage of exports from the underdeveloped world (Latin
America and other), the significance of which will be pointed

out later when we discuss the issue of financial dependency of underdeveloped countries.

The impact of these overseas sales from direct investment is what was no doubt in the mind of the investment banker who wrote in a recent article in *Foreign Affairs*:

The role of U.S. direct investment in the world economy is staggering. According to the U.S. Council of the International Chamber of Commerce, the gross value of production by American companies abroad is well in excess of $100 billion a year. That is to say, on the basis of the gross value of their output, U.S. enterprises abroad in the aggregate comprise the third largest country (if such a term can be used to designate these companies) in the world—with a gross product greater than that of any country except the United States and the Soviet Union. Of course, these enterprises are large users of raw materials and components produced locally, so that their contribution to the net product (values added) is much less than their gross sales.[42]

As far as manufacturing is concerned, the huge foreign business operation is mainly concentrated in Canada and Europe, as can be seen from Table XI. And since the Second World

TABLE XI
DIRECT FOREIGN INVESTMENT IN MANUFACTURING
(*Million $*)

	1950		1966	
	Dollars	Percent of Total	Dollars	Percent of Total
All Areas	$3,831	100%	$22,050	100%
Selected Areas				
Canada	1,897	49.5	7,674	34.8
Mexico	133	3.5	797	3.6
Argentina	161	4.2	652	3.0
Brazil	285	7.4	846	3.8
Europe	932	24.3	8,879	40.3
South Africa	44	1.1	271	1.2
India	16	0.4	118	0.5
Japan	5	0.1	333	1.5
Philippines	23	0.6	180	0.8
Australia	98	2.6	999	4.5

Source: Department of Commerce, *United States Business Investment in Foreign Countries,* Washington, D.C., 1960, and Walther Lederer and Frederick Cutler, *International Investments of the United States in 1966* in *Survey of Current Business,* September, 1967.

War, in an environment influenced by the Marshall Plan and
NATO, the main trend has been the flow of manufacturing
capital to Europe.[43]

But the United States is not the only contender for these
markets. The cross currents of investment, as a reflection of
the competition among giant corporations for markets, is shown
in Table XII. English firms invest in France and West Germany. Belgium invests in France, West Germany, and England.
Obviously, however, the position of the United States as a
foreign investor in Europe is overwhelming. As might be expected, the concentration of investment by a small number of
giant firms has resulted in the United States firms' having
quite impressive shares of the market in particular industries

TABLE XII
THE AMERICAN SHARE IN THE STOCK OF
FOREIGN INVESTMENT

	France 1962	West Germany 1964	Britain 1962
United States	45%	34%	72%
Great Britain	12	10	—
Netherlands	11	17	2
Switzerland	5	16	7
Belgium	8	5	1
France	—	7	2
Sweden	1	3	1
Italy	5	included in "others"	1
West Germany	3	—	1
Canada	2	included in "others"	9
Others	8	8	4
Total	100%	100%	100%

Source: Christopher Layton, *Trans-Atlantic Investments,* Boulogne-sur-
Seine, France, The Atlantic Institute, 1966, p. 13.

in Europe. Observe from Table XIII that United States firms
control over half of the automobile industry in Britain, close to
40 percent of petroleum in Germany, and over 40 percent of
the telegraphic, telephone, electronic, and statistical equipment
business in France (the control of computing machines in
France is 75 percent).

TABLE XIII
ESTIMATES OF U.S. SHARE IN CERTAIN INDUSTRIES

France 1963

	U.S. Firms (percent of sales)
Petroleum refining	20%
Razor blades & safety razors	87
Cars	13
Tires	over 30
Carbon black	95
Refrigerators	25
Machine tools	20
Semi-conductors	25
Washing machines	27
Lifts & elevators	30
Tractors & agricultural machinery	35
Telegraphic & telephone equipment	42
Electronic & statistical machines (of which computers 75%)	43
Sewing machines	70
Electric razors	60
Accounting machines	75

Britain 1964

	U.S. Firms (percent of sales)
Refined petroleum products	over 40%
Computers	over 40
Cars	over 50
Carbon black	over 75
Refrigerators	33⅓% to 50
Pharmaceuticals	over 20
Tractors & agricultural machinery	over 40
Instruments	over 15
Razor blades & safety razors	Approx. 55

West Germany

	U.S. Firms (percent of capital)
Petroleum	38%
Machinery, vehicles, metal products (of which cars 40%)	15
Food industry	7
Chemicals, rubber, etc.	3
Electrical, optics, toys, musical (of which computers 84%)	10

Source: Christopher Layton, *Trans-Atlantic Investments,* Boulogne-sur-Seine, France, The Atlantic Institute, 1966, p. 19.

The tie-in between monopolistic trends and the flow of investment to Europe is indicated by the following: in the three biggest European markets (West Germany, Britain, and France) 40 percent of United States direct investment is accounted for by three firms—Esso, General Motors, and Ford. In all Western Europe, 20 United States firms account for two thirds of United States investment.[44] Between 1950 and 1965 "more and more of the major companies have bought or built their way into Europe. By 1961, 460 of the 1000 largest U.S. companies had a subsidiary or branch in Europe. By 1965, the figure had risen to 700 out of 1000."[45]

In short, the internationalization of capital among the giant firms is of a much higher order today than was the case fifty years ago when Lenin wrote his work on imperialism.

NOTES

1. *The New Cambridge Modern History* (F. H. Hinsley, ed.), Cambridge, England, 1962, Vol. XI, pp. 2-3.
2. The discussion on technology is based on the following: Thorstein Veblen, *Absentee Ownership*, New York, 1923, Chapter X ("The Technology of Physics and Chemistry").; Geoffrey Barraclough, *An Introduction to Contemporary History*, Baltimore, 1967; David S. Landes, "Technological Change and Development in Western Europe," in *The Cambridge Economic History of Europe* (H. J. Habakkuk and M. Postan, eds.), Cambridge, England, 1965, Vol. VI, Part I; J. D. Bernal, *Science in History*, London, 1954; C. Singer, E. J. Holmyard, A. R. Hall and Trevor J. Williams, *A History of Technology*, Oxford, 1958, Vol. V.
3. Abbott Payson Usher, "The Industrialization of Modern Britain" in *Technology and Culture*, Spring, 1960, pp. 119-120.
4. William Ashworth, *A Short History of the International Economy Since 1850*, London, 1964, p. 22.
5. Alfred D. Chandler, Jr., "The Beginnings of 'Big Business' in American History" in *The Business History Review*, Spring, 1959, reprinted in *Pivotal Interpretations of American History* (Carl N. Degler, ed.), New York, 1966, Vol. II, pp. 109-110.
6. Along with the growing role of the investment banker was the increased use of the stock market for industrial securities. Before 1880, the stock exchanges dealt almost exclusively in railroad and bank securities. Until the late 1880's industrial companies remained too small and too little known to speculators. It was not until 1890-1893, at the start of the major concentration and merger drive, that industrial securities began

to be listed on the stock exchange and to be traded by leading brokerage houses. See Thomas R. Navin and Marian V. Sears, "The Rise of a Market for Industrial Securities, 1887-1902" in *The Business History Review,* June, 1955, pp. 105-138. See also Gabriel Kolko, *The Triumph of Conservatism,* Chicago, 1963, Chapter 1.

7. Geoffrey Barraclough, *op. cit.,* p. 54.

8. Based on A. J. Youngson, "The Opening Up of New Territories" in *The Cambridge Economic History of Europe,* Cambridge, England, 1965, Vol. VI, Part I.

9. *The New Cambridge Modern History,* Cambridge, England, 1962, Vol. XI, p. 5.

10. *Ibid.,* p. 6.

11. A. J. Youngson, *op. cit.*

12. Same as fn. 9, p. 52.

13. *Ibid.,* p. 6. As an historical reference point for this commercial revolution, note that the Suez Canal and the first transcontinental railway in America are opened up in 1869.

14. "There was some diminution in the size of armies in the period of tranquility after 1815, but after 1870 there was, among the great powers, a steady growth in the size and cost of armies and navies." Quincy Wright, *A Study of War,* Chicago, 1942, Vol. I, p. 233. Per capita defense appropriations in 1880 in the United States were $1.03; in 1900, $2.53; in 1914, $3.20. *Ibid.,* Vol. I, p. 671.

15. For excellent historical studies of the development of imperialist patterns in American history, see William Appleman Williams, *The Contours of American History,* Cleveland, 1961 (especially the section, "The Age of Corporation Capitalism: 1882-   ); Walter La Feber, *The New Empire, An Interpretation of American Expansion, 1860-1898,* Ithaca, New York, 1963; and Thomas J. McCormick, *China Market, America's Quest for Informal Empire, 1893-1901,* Chicago, 1967.

16. Note that giant U.S. corporations learned early in the game the desirability of controlling their raw material supplies. Vertical integration, including control over the mining of their own raw materials, was characteristic of the giants in oil, fertilizer, steel, copper, paper, explosives, and other industries. See Alfred D. Chandler, *op. cit.*

17. When Lenin gives his explanation of the transformation from competition to monopoly, he notes: "Concentration has reached the point at which it is possible to make an approximate estimate of all sources of raw materials (for example, the iron ore deposits) of a country and even, as we shall see, of several countries, or of the whole world. Not only are such estimates made, but these sources are captured by gigantic monopolist combines." *Imperialism, The Highest Stage of Capitalism,* New York, 1939, p. 25. Later in the essay: "Finance capital is not only interested in the already known sources of raw materials; it is also interested in the potential sources of raw materials, because present-day technical development is extremely rapid, and because land which is useless today may be made fertile tomorrow if new methods are applied . . . and large amounts of capital are invested." *Ibid.,* p. 83.

18. Mira Wilkins and Frank Ernest Hill, *American Business Abroad, Ford on Six Continents,* Detroit, 1964, p. 1.

19. Matthew Simon and David E. Novack, "Some Dimensions of the

American Commercial Invasion of Europe, 1871-1914: An Introductory Essay," in *Journal of Economic History*, December, 1964, Table 2.

20. Note also: "The composition of manufactured exports has been changing ceaselessly since 1879 in a fairly consistent direction—away from products of animal or vegetable origin and toward those of mineral origin. Among those of mineral origin, the trend has been away from commodities closely tied to the production of raw materials, such as petroleum products, to metal products, including machinery and vehicles; and within the metal products group the shift has been to the more complex machinery and vehicles." Robert E. Lipsey, *Price and Quantity Trends in the Foreign Trade of the United States*, Princeton, 1963, pp. 59-60.

21. *Op. cit.*, p. 62.

22. It is customary to think of competition and monopoly as direct opposites. This is quite proper according to dictionary definitions. However, in Marxist literature, the terms competition and monopoly are used to designate different phases of capitalist society. In neither of these phases is there either pure competition or pure monopoly. Indeed, it is the very essence of the theory of imperialism to recognize that competition exists within the monopoly phase. Competition is between giants of the same industry (within and outside the nation) and between industries (steel vs. aluminum vs. plastics, for example).

23. Thus, all the iron material for India's railroads was imported from England. Even in the United States, which had a growing iron industry, iron rails were imported from England. South Wales iron masters took part of their payment for this iron in the form of bonds of the railroad companies.

24. *Korea, Determined Strides Forward*, The Chase Manhattan Bank, May, 1967, p. 3.

25. For a critique of the "surplus capital" abstraction and suggestions for more significant analysis of current developments, see Paul A. Baran and Paul M. Sweezy, "Notes on the Theory of Imperialism" in *Problems of Economic Dynamics and Planning, Essays in Honour of Michal Kalecki*, Oxford, 1966. Reprinted in MONTHLY REVIEW, March, 1966.

26. It is one of the significant ironies of these times that the wave of protectionism followed on the heels of the widespread adoption of the international gold standard. "The agrarian crisis and the Great Depression of 1873-86 had shaken confidence in economic self-healing. From now onward the typical institutions of market economy could usually be introduced only if accompanied by protectionist measures, all the more so because since the late 1870's and early 1880's nations were forming themselves into organized units which were apt to suffer grievously from the dislocations involved in any sudden adjustment to the needs of foreign trade or foreign exchanges. The supreme vehicle of the expansion of market economy, the gold standard, was thus usually accompanied by the simultaneous introduction of the typical protectionist policies of the age such as social legislation and customs tariffs." Karl Polanyi, *The Great Transformation*, Boston, 1957, p. 214.

27. For documentation and analysis see George W. F. Hallgarten, *Imperialismus Vor 1914*, Munich, 1963; and Herbert Feis, *Europe The World's Banker, 1870-1914*, New York, 1965.

28. On the question of uneven rate of development: "Thus, Great

Britain stood in much the same relation to most of the regions of Europe around 1850 that Europe and the United States bore to the Orient and South America a half century later." L. H. Jenks, *The Migration of British Capital to 1875,* New York, 1927, pp. 187-188.

29. Lenin, *op cit.,* p. 85. It is noteworthy that Lenin specifically rejects the definition advocated by Karl Kautsky which confines imperialism to the acquisition of raw materials supplying colonies; that is, the attempt by industrialized capitalist countries to control and annex agrarian regions. He debates this point in terms of the conditions existing prior to and during World War I: "The characteristic feature of imperialism is precisely that it strives to annex *not only* agricultural regions, but even highly industrialized regions (German appetite for Belgium; French appetite for Lorraine), because (1) the fact that the world is already divided up obliges those contemplating a *new* division to reach out for *any kind* of territory, and (2) because an essential feature of imperialism is the rivalry between a number of great powers in the striving for hegemony, i.e., for the conquest of territory, not so much directly for themselves as to weaken the adversary and undermine *his* hegemony. (Belgium is chiefly necessary to Germany as a base for operations against England; England needs Baghdad as a base for operations against Germany, etc.)" *Ibid.,* pp. 91-92.

30. We are referring here naturally to the main drift. France's attempt to break out of the close ties of the U.S. international system is one example of strain. Another example of potential strain is the program of important groups in West Germany to create a true political bloc in Europe which, on the one hand, can compete more effectively with the U.S. and, on the other hand, can be used to pull back some of Eastern European socialist countries (notably East Germany—but others as well) into their own imperialist "associations." These tensions are involved in the maneuvering with respect to the international gold exchange and dollar system, which will be discussed later in the article.

31. This and the preceding quotes are from Department of State *Bulletin,* May 10, 1965, p. 695.

32. *The Economist,* London, January 27, 1968.

33. For the background information on this, see Robert Engler, *The Politics of Oil,* New York, 1961; and Harvey O'Connor, *The Empire of Oil,* New York, 1955. The clearest demonstration of the role of politics is found in the acquisition by the United States of oil reserves in Iran after the CIA-directed overturn of Prime Minister Mossadegh. Before the nationalization by Mossadegh of the British-owned Anglo-Iranian Company, U.S. firms could not break through this British preserve. After the overturn, five U.S. firms—Standard of New Jersey, Socony, Standard of California, Texaco, and Gulf—obtained 40 percent of the oil interest previously held by Anglo-Iranian. For the details on this, see Chapter 8, "The Blending of Public and Private Abroad," in the above-mentioned book by Engler, and Chapter 31, "The Threat from Iran," in O'Connor's book.

34. Same as fn. 31, p. 700.

35. Hans H. Landsberg, *Natural Resources for U.S. Growth,* Baltimore, 1964, p. 206.

36. The Commission on Foreign Economic Policy, *Staff Papers Presented to the Commission,* Washington, D.C., February, 1954, p. 224.

37. International Development Advisory Board, *Partners in Progress,*

Washington, D.C., March, 1951, p. 46.

38. The President's Materials Policy Commission, *Resources for Freedom*, Washington, D.C., June, 1952, Vol. IV, *The Promise of Technology*, p. 11.

39. Address at the Gettysburgh College Convocation, April 4, 1959, in Public Papers of the Presidents of the United States, *Dwight D. Eisenhower 1959*, Washington, D.C., 1960, p. 314.

40. Rockefeller Brothers Fund, *Foreign Economic Policy for the Twentieth Century*, Garden City, New York, 1958, p. 11 for the first item, p. 16 for the second.

41. Subcommittee on Foreign Economic Policy of the Joint Economic Committee, Congress of the United States, 84th Congress, 2nd Session, *Hearings*, December 10, 12, and 13, 1956, pp. 127, 131.

42. Leo Model, "The Politics of Private Foreign Investment," in *Foreign Affairs*, July, 1967, pp. 640-641.

43. A frequently met explanation for the upsurge in U.S. investment in Europe is the special attraction of the European Economic Community (Common Market). This is contradicted in an analysis by Anthony Scaperlanda: ". . . the general assumption that the E.E.C.'s creation would cause a reallocation of international investment is not supported by the empirical data. Instead, the non-E.E.C. area has either maintained or increased its share of United States direct investment in Western Europe." "The E.E.C. and U.S. Foreign Investment: Some Empirical Evidence," in *The Economic Journal*, March, 1967, p. 26.

44. Christopher Layton, *Trans-Atlantic Investment*, Boulogne-sur-Seine, France, 1966, p. 18.

45. *Ibid.*, p. 18.

3

THE FINANCIAL NETWORK

U.S. Banking Goes International

A recent article in *Fortune* reports: "The biggest growth area of United States banking today is not in the United States but overseas. . . . The expansion overseas is also creating the first truly international network of banks."[1] This development in banking is a fitting complement to the new role of the United States as the leader and organizer of the imperialist order. What could be more natural than the coincidence of (a) the widespread military and political presence of the United States around the globe (via wars, military bases, and military and economic aid); (b) the dominant position of United States capital in the creation of multinational industrial empires; (c) the evolution of the dollar as the key international medium of payments, credit, and reserves; and (d) the growth of multinational banking?

The banking community is of course well aware of these relations. A report issued by Brown Brothers Harriman & Co. notes: "Politically the United States has vital interests in almost every quarter of the globe. It is not unnatural to expect commercial interests to follow and indeed they are encouraged to do so."[2]

As a concrete example, this interrelationship of trade and flag can be seen in the establishment of United States banking in Saigon. A *New York Times* story in 1965, reporting that the two largest United States banks were seeking branches in South Vietnam, quotes a First National City Bank vice president,

Henry Sperry, as saying:

Afterward you'll have a major job of reconstruction. . . . That will take financing, and financing means banks.

It would be illogical to permit the English and the French to monopolize the banking business, because South Vietnam's economy is becoming more and more United States oriented.[3]

Two U.S. banks were in fact opened in Saigon in the summer of 1966. As seen by *Business Week*:

In the midst of a neighborhood of honky-tonk GI bars, the Saigon branches of Bank of America and Chase Manhattan Bank look like modern fortresses in granite and sandstone. . . . The banks . . . were built especially for wartime conditions—glass blocks instead of windows, and walls designed to withstand mine explosions and mortar attacks. . . . If it weren't for the massive U.S. presence there, probably neither bank would be in Vietnam. The banks came into the Vietnam picture last year as a result of the big U.S. buildup that began in 1965. The U.S. government wanted a place to keep funds—for the Embassy, the Agency for International Development, and the military. And it saw no reason to help French or other foreign banks in the country.[4]

This consideration of the banks for the government and of the government for the banks is not restricted to times of war. Thus, when the United States disposes of surplus agricultural stocks by selling them for foreign currencies, large sums of money accumulate to the account of the United States in the buyer countries. What better opportunity to give a helping hand to a deserving bank seeking a foothold in an underdeveloped country? A new bank needs a source of deposits to start its financial ball rolling. In Pakistan, for example:

Most of the banks receiving these deposits [of United States-owned local currencies] have been privately owned United States commercial banks in Pakistan (e.g. Bank of America, American Express, and others). Due to the fact that these banks are relatively new in Pakistan and, therefore, not well established, they have as yet relatively little contact with the industrial and commercial sectors as compared with the older and better established Pakistani or British-owned commercial banks. The American banks are, therefore, eager to get these funds and they are most likely to re-lend them on the interbank call market.[5]

Thus, the United States government does its bit to give a

helping hand to United States banks operating overseas. The bankers, themselves, however, are not laggards in seizing the new opportunities and shouldering their world mission. In a review of the new aspects of international banking, George S. Moore, president of the First National City Bank, described recently the accelerated pace of international finance—the rapid increase in loans to foreigners and the deposits by foreigners in New York banks—and observed that such a heightened pace of activity points toward "an international interdependence unprecedented since the emergence of the nation-state. American banks have already responded to these developments. With the dollar the leading international currency and the United States the world's largest exporter and importer of goods, services, and capital, it is only natural that the United States banks gird themselves *to play the same relative role in international finance that the great British financial institutions played in the nineteenth century*."[6] (Emphasis added.)

This is hardly a modest ambition. The world supremacy of British banking was not, after all, a matter of will power or mere technical competence, but part and parcel of Britain's monopoly over international trade and its primacy as a colonial power. Until the 1880's, British banks had virtually no competition in financing of international trade outside the continent of Europe. In the latter decades of the 19th century, German and French systems of foreign banks began to duplicate the spread of British banks, except in regions under the British flag.[7] Yet, despite the growing competition, England's dominance in the financing of foreign trade persisted. In fact, in the late 19th and early 20th century most of United States foreign trade—and most of international trade originating elsewhere—was financed not with dollars but in sterling by London banks.[8]

The inhibitions imposed by the British international network of finance on the potential external economic expansion of the United States was well recognized and much discussed as the pressure for external expansion grew more intense. William Adams Brown, a close student of financial aspects of this period, commented:

For at least a decade before the passage of the Federal Reserve Act [1913] ways and means of promoting American export trade in manufactured goods had been actively discussed in the United States. Among these were the extension of the foreign facilities of American banks and the creation of an acceptance market in New York. There had been an increasing desire to provide American exporters with facilities in foreign countries comparable to those built up during the nineteenth century by British banks and during the latter part of the nineteenth century and the first part of the twentieth century by German, Italian and other foreign banks. . . . Though the facilities of this system [of British banks] provided American commerce with cheap and efficient financing, the increasingly competitive nature of American exports of manufactures rendered dependence on these foreign facilities distasteful to those engaged in an aggressive expansion of American trade. There was a strong feeling that the use of sterling acceptance was a handicap to American trade because it strengthened the preference for British goods already built up by long standing connections and by British controlled enterprises throughout the world. . . . From the day on which the war [the First World War] broke out Americans began to lay the foundation for an extension of American banking abroad and therefore for the provision, at the points of origin of foreign business, of a supply of bills drawn under American credits. The war did not lay the foundation for this movement, but it swept away the obstacles that had impeded its development.[9]

The obstacles that stood in the way could be traced in the main to the entrenched position previously attained by other strong industrial nations and the preferred position they had in their extensive colonial possessions. The United States, which up to the First World War was a debtor nation, had not had a sufficient degree of financial freedom to cope with the competitive edge achieved by the extension of international banking and investment of other nations. What hurt most was the lead taken by European business and finance on the doorsteps of the United States—in Latin America. An official of the National City Bank of New York explained in 1915:

The South American foreign banks and their branches [of British and German banks] are active agencies for the promotion of trade relations between the South American republics and the home countries. These banks have entered actively into the industrial and economical lives of the communities in which they are located. They have furnished money for the development of the resources of these countries; have financed railroads, harbor works, public utilities, and warehouses. They have been instrumental in building up markets at home for the raw materials produced by South America, and have in this manner established a basis for a reciprocal exchange of products. The money of England and Germany has been freely invested in the future of these countries. England and Germany have put into Argentine, Brazil, and Uruguay, in the last twenty-five years, approximately four thousand million dollars, and as a result enjoy together 46 percent of the total trade of these three countries.[10]

The war raging in Europe helped to stimulate the vision of this banker:

A rare combination of circumstances now favors us. The business ties between other great nations whose commercial intercourse has long been reciprocal and friendly have been sundered at the very moment of the creation of the machinery so badly needed for building up of our foreign commerce. Considering the fundamental readjustments in trade relations between many nations that are bound to result from the conflict now raging, the opportunity presents itself to this country to construct in the next few years a lasting foundation for a profitable foreign commerce of large proportions.[11]

The machinery referred to was the creation of the legal framework, through the Federal Reserve Act, for the extension of United States branch banks into foreign lands. It is understandable that a banker seeking new business and profit opportunities should be enthusiastic about the opening of doors to the rest of the world. But banking business abroad, as within the country, is not an independent operation. It lives and grows in symbiotic relation with expanding foreign investment and foreign trade, as outlined by the National City Bank official:

In order to build up a profitable and lasting commerce in hitherto untouched markets in foreign countries, it will be necessary for us to aid in the development of those countries. Brazil, Colombia, Argentine, Chile, Peru, and other of the South American republics have natural resources of greatest value awaiting development. If in the years to come the United States shall invest its surplus capital in the upbuilding of South America along the same lines which govern the investment of European countries in that field, trade opportunities will result which will show a return to us of many times the original investment.[12]

This projected course of development was of course pursued, at first mainly in Latin America but extended step-by-step to other areas of the world. The foreign branches of United States banks did in fact become an important instrument for the movement of this surplus capital and for the exploration of new trade markets. The war-induced reshuffle of finance and trade provided the setting for a major push forward of foreign banking and investment. However, it took another world war, the "open door" created by the break-up of the old colonial system, and the ascendancy of the United States to "free world" leadership before United States banking became full-blown international banking.

Branch Banks Straddle the World Capitalist Market

United States banks enter foreign markets in three ways:

(1) By use of foreign banks as correspondent banks. The latter handle the overseas transactions for the United States bank. This activity is often supplemented by setting up offices in selected foreign cities, from which bank representatives facilitate overseas bank business. While such outposts are useful to bankers, their operations are limited since they do not engage in full banking operations such as making loans.

(2) By setting up branches which carry on full banking operations as they would in the United States. These activities are naturally adapted to such banking laws as exist in the host country.

(3) By setting up subsidiary corporations. These corporations buy into foreign-owned banks, set up bank and finance companies abroad, and invest in a wide variety of non-banking businesses.

While correspondent banks and overseas offices are helpful devices for servicing United States customers, it is the system of branch banks which opens up significant new business and profit opportunities. It is the branch banks that can reap special profits from United States international activities; the money spent by United States armed forces abroad, the bank deposits arising from foreign aid, and the banking business that accompanies private investment abroad.

It is the branch banks which provide the medium for getting a share of the world's financial business—by competing with local institutions and with the agencies of other international banking systems. Finally, they are the media through which the special economic strength of the especially large banks can be wielded to become even wealthier and more influential. For just as it is the largest manufacturing, mining, and oil firms that are paramount in overseas investment, so in the banking field expansion is concentrated in the largest United States banks. Thus, of the 298 overseas branches as of the end of 1967, 259 are owned by three banks: First National City Bank, Chase Manhattan Bank, and Bank of America.[18]

The growth pattern of foreign branch banks—and especially the feverish expansion of recent years—can be seen by an examination of Tables XIV and XV. Table XIV shows the number of countries in which branch banks were operating in selected years in five major areas as well as in United States overseas areas and trust territories. In 1918, United States banks had established branches in sixteen countries, primarily in Latin America and in Europe. Remember that such operations were insignificant for United States banks prior to the First World War. In fact, only state-chartered banks were legally competent to open branches abroad. National banks did not get the go-ahead signal until the Federal Reserve Act of 1913. The pace of expansion during the 20's and 30's was fairly slow, but it is noteworthy in the light of more recent developments that this period is marked by entrance into the Far East. The decline in the number of countries represented in Europe between 1918 and 1939 is due to the elimination of branches in Russia and Germany.

There was obviously little change during the war years, except for the closing down of branches in enemy and enemy-occupied territories. A new rise, still at a relatively slow rate, is resumed after the war, until about 1955. After that, the pace quickens. By 1960, branches are to be found in every major area. At the end of 1967, branches are located in 55 different countries outside the United States.

The expansion shown is influenced by several factors: (1) the continued extension of United States foreign oil, mining, and manufacturing interests; (2) the spread of military bases; and (3) the penetration of areas by government military and economic aid, including entrance into former colonies which once had been the exclusive preserve of the owning country.

TABLE XIV

NUMBER OF COUNTRIES OUTSIDE THE UNITED STATES IN WHICH U.S. BANKS HAVE BRANCHES

	1918	1939	1950	1955	1960	1967
Latin America [a]	10	11	10	10	13	22
Europe	5	3	4	4	4	10
Africa	0	0	0	3	1	3
Near East	0	0	0	0	3	3
Far East	0	6	7	6	8	12
U.S. Overseas Areas and Trust Territories [b]	1	2	3	3	4	5
Total	16	22	24	26	33	55

(a) Includes Western European dependencies.
(b) Canal Zone, Guam, Puerto Rico, Truk Islands, and Virgin Islands. Data for the Philippines are included in the Far East, even though this country was a dependency for some of these years.

Source:　Board of Governors of the Federal Reserve System, *Annual Report* for the relevant years for data up to 1960. Data for 1967 from mimeographed list prepared by the Federal Reserve Board, *Overseas Branches of Corporations Engaged in Foreign Banking and Financing in Operation on December 31, 1967*. The data for 1967 include three subsidiary banks of First National City Bank which are not included in the 1967 tabulation of the Federal Reserve System *Annual Report*. Excluded are overseas fiduciary affiliates and banking facilities at military establishments provided through arrangements made by the Treasury Department with banks designated as depositaries and financial agents.

Immediately after the war, United States banking returned to Germany. By 1950, United States branches had been opened for the first time in Singapore, Thailand, and Guam. The next move was to the Near East. Between 1950 and 1955, branches were established in Egypt, Lebanon, and Saudi Arabia. In following years, branch banks covered the whole complex of

United States political and military operations: Nigeria, Malaysia, Okinawa, Korea, Taiwan, Vietnam, Morocco, Liberia, Guyana, Trinidad, Jamaica, and others.

The geographic spread of branch banking abroad is only one phase of international involvement. For, as a branch bank becomes well entrenched in a country, sub-branches and new branches tend to be added throughout the country. Thus, as can be seen from Table XV, the increase in the number of branches abroad is much more extensive than the number of countries in which United States banks are to be found. During the 21-year period from 1918 to 1939, the net increase in branches was 28. (The gross increase was larger than indicated, since during this period 11 branches of the National City Bank located in Russia disappeared via nationalization.[14]) This

TABLE XV
NUMBER OF U.S. BANK BRANCHES
OUTSIDE THE UNITED STATES

	1918[c]	1939	1950	1955	1960	1967
Latin America [a]	31	47	49	56	55 [e]	134
Europe	26	16	15	17	19	59
Africa	0	0	0	4	1	4
Near East	0	0	0	0	4	7
Far East	0	18	19 [d]	20	23	63
U.S. Overseas Areas and Trust Territories [b]	4	8	12	14	22	31
Total	61	89	95	111	124	298

(a) Same as Table XIV.
(b) Same as Table XIV.
(c) These are the branches authorized by the Board of Governors of the Federal Reserve System up to 1918. Included are 11 branches of the National City Bank in Russia prior to the nationalization of banks by the U.S.S.R.
(d) This increase occurs despite the elimination of United States branch banks in China. Of the 18 branches in the Far East in 1939, 7 were located in China. Hong Kong is counted here as a separate country.
(e) Excluded are 21 branch banks nationalized by the Cuban Government in 1960.

Source: Same as Table XIV.

pace of expansion, obviously influenced by the decline in business opportunities during the Great Depression, was vastly accelerated after the end of the Second World War. Sixteen foreign branches were added in the five years from 1950 to 1955. From 1955 to 1967, over 180 new branches were opened. Note also that by 1967 there were more branch banks in the Far East than in Europe.

While United States banks are spreading out through the underdeveloped countries, with almost half their branches in Latin America, their influence in the industrialized countries is also becoming increasingly strategic. *Fortune* observes that "It has become a cliché in banking circles to say that 'the only really European banks nowadays are American.' "[15] And according to Professor Kindleberger, "It is worth noting that of the commercial banks it is the United States institutions—Morgan Guaranty Trust Co., Chase Manhattan, First National City, in particular—which are represented in the several countries of the Common Market rather than European institutions."[16]

The business economics behind the upsurge of foreign banking is similar to the motives behind the movement of industry abroad: a relative shrinkage of business opportunities on the domestic front and the attractive profit opportunities overseas. As one analyst put it:

American bankers intensified their efforts in the international area for two reasons. First, many of them have come to believe that their domestic markets offer limited room for further significant growth. . . . A second reason for going international is the seemingly limitless demand for international banking and financial services.[17]

Very little information is publicly available at this time on the size of this new business compared to domestic activities. The *Fortune* article referred to above pulls together some bits and pieces:

In those ten years [prior to 1967], deposits in the foreign branches of New York banks have risen from $1.35 billion to $9.5 billion; lately they have been growing at a rate seven times greater than deposits at home. At Manufacturers Hanover, foreign business has increased from 10 percent to 25 percent of total business. Three years ago, Chase Manhattan disclosed that 14 percent of its net profits came from foreign business, and that percentage has certainly risen since. Manufacturers Hanover says that the profits of its international division have more than doubled in the last five years, which probably means that earnings have kept pace with the division's growing business.[18]

Foreign Expansion Via Bank Subsidiaries

The acceleration of foreign branch banking indicates only one aspect of the upsurge of banking activities abroad. The other dynamic vehicle used by U.S. banks to penetrate the arteries of international finance is the subsidiary corporation.

The door to this technique was also opened by one of the first reforms of the Wilson administration—the Federal Reserve Act—as a method of permitting and encouraging the foreign expansion of banks. The door was opened wider by the 1919 amendment to the Federal Reserve Act, known as the Edge Act. In effect, these legislative enactments permitted United States banks to set up subsidiary corporations (a) to facilitate the creation of branches in countries which have laws prohibiting branch banks, and (b) to enable banks to engage in a wider range of foreign financial and investment activities. These subsidiary corporations were enabled to go beyond the usual financial activities of domestic banks, including direct investment in non-financial operations—such as manufacturing, mining, and trade which banks are prohibited from doing in the United States.

While the groundwork for such corporations was laid during the First World War and its aftermath, they did not get a firm grip until the 1950's. Part of the reason for their early difficulties was that quite a few of them got started just as the 1920-1921 crisis broke out. The instability of world prices complicated their operations. Moreover, the lack of experienced and trained personnel acted as a drawback. The banks did not have a large reserve of experienced colonial administrators to draw from, as did the British. And, while the war had given the United States dollar and United States banking a big boost, it was still only a competitor for world financial leadership: the entrenched British financial network, supported by its colonial empire and widespread military organization, presented a formidable obstacle to the aspirations of United States finance on the world scene.

Finally, this form of foreign penetration suffered a major setback during the world-wide depression of the 1930's. In 1929, United States banks owned 18 such subsidiary corporations; by 1945, after depression and war, only two of these corporations survived.

The contrasting developments of the 1950's and 1960's is an instructive illustration of the changes in foreign finance that have accompanied the new position of the United States in its political, military, and economic operations. In this latest period, these subsidiary corporations have mushroomed into an effective and pervasive instrument, and by all signs are still on the increase. The pattern of growth is shown in Table XVI.

TABLE XVI

NUMBER OF SUBSIDIARY CORPORATIONS IN INTERNATIONAL BANKING

1929	18
1945	2
1956	7
1960	15
1963	35
1967	52

Note:　Edge Act and Agreement Corporations are combined. These terms refer to technical differences depending on whether the corporations are organized under Section 25 or Section 25(a) of the Federal Reserve Act.

Source:　1929 and 1945—"Banking Goes International," *Business Conditions* (Federal Reserve Board of Chicago), April 1967. 1956, 1960, and 1963—"Edge Act and Agreement Corporations in International Banking and Finance," *Monthly Review* (Federal Reserve Bank of New York), May 1964. 1967—Federal Reserve Board, *Overseas Branches and Corporations Engaged in Foreign Banking and Financing in Operation on December 31, 1967* (mimeographed list).

The manifold operations of these subsidiary corporations can be summarized in three categories:

(1) Banking and financing companies have been established in Canada, 7 European countries, 8 Latin American countries, and 2 African countries.[19] These companies in turn carry on a variety of investing activities, often in cooperation with local banks, other international bankers, and at times with the United States government. (Note: these are in addition to the branches listed in Tables XIV and XV.)

(2) The subsidiary corporations are used as vehicles to buy up minority or controlling interests in banks abroad. This enables them to get a foothold in the banking system of a country, as for example through the controlling interest held by a Bank of America subsidiary in Banca d'America e d'Italia (Milan), the ninth largest commercial bank in Italy operating with a network of more than 70 branches.[20] It also enables them to reach into the networks of international banks of other industrialized nations, banks which in the past had had the special opportunities of sinking roots in their country's colonial possessions. For example: a Chase Manhattan Bank subsidiary owns 15 percent of the London-based Standard Bank, which in turn has an extensive network of African and Latin American banks; The Morgan Guaranty Trust subsidiary has holdings in commercial, development, and investment banks in 24 countries; a First National City Bank subsidiary has a 40 percent interest in Banque Internationale pour L'Afrique Occidentale, which in turn operates 41 branches in Africa.[21]

(3) The subsidiaries are used to obtain ownership in a wide variety of industrial and service undertakings abroad, especially in the underdeveloped countries. In part, this is done by including a stock conversion feature in the loans extended.[22] This means that the bank can, under the terms of the loan, convert part or all of the loan into an equity holding—an attractive contingency if the enterprise turns out to be unusually profitable. Not that the bank corporation fails to make a nice profit on the loans themselves. The 1962 Brown Brothers Harriman & Co. report notes, "Suffice it to say that life for the Edge Act banker [one type of subsidiary] begins at something well above the customary 6 percent of his domestic cousins."[23]

In addition, these corporations make direct investments in

a wide variety of industries abroad. David Rockefeller, president of The Chase Manhattan Bank, describes the activities of one of his bank's subsidiaries, Chase International Investment Corporation (CIIC), thus:

CIIC, which has now been in full operation for about ten years, is currently involved in some 30 projects in 20 different countries. These projects range from a textile mill in Nigeria to a tin mining operation in Bolivia, and include such other diverse activities as a steel mill in Turkey, a paper mill in Guatemala, and an equipment leasing company in Mexico.[24]

Thus far, we have described one aspect of the internationalization of United States finance—the build-up of a network of branches and subsidiary corporations for investment abroad. But it should be understood that this is only part of the internationalization process—a process which finds its focus in the transfer of the central international capital market from Europe to the United States and the enthronement of the dollar as the major world currency.

The Dollar as the World Currency: New York as the World Banker

The late Professor Schumpeter, if memory serves, once remarked that the money market is the headquarters of the capitalist system. It was undoubtedly in this sense that the United States assumption of leadership of the capitalist world coincided with New York City's becoming the undisputed center of international finance, and the United States dollar's becoming the international currency of the capitalist world.

The previous center of the world money market was The City—a square mile in London containing the Bank of England, the gold market, the international insurance market, leading commodity exchanges, and the head offices of the major banks. It was backed up by the conquest of the seas, the world's largest merchant marine fleet, the world's largest colonial empire, and the domination of international trade. In arguing against the romantic notion still held by some in England about restoring its old glory, the Oxford economist, Dr. Thomas Balogh, reminds us that

the rise of London to the center of an international economy was based on Britain's *mercantile supremacy* as an Imperial Power and her *industrial leadership* as an initiator of mechanized mass production. It was this double superiority which enabled London to become the world center for short- and long-term finance, and added further cumulative gains. The play of the Gold Standard became a source of profit and actively contributed to maintaining the British balance of payments.[25]

The financial advantage England achieved through this process still gives sustenance to England even after it has descended to the rank of a secondary power. In 1966 Lord Comer, the Governor of the Bank of England, testified to this in the following terms:

I think we have to recognize the extent to which the British standard of living is dependent today, as it has been throughout this century, on our invisible earnings, particularly on our investment income from overseas. The figures speak for themselves. The origin of our overseas investments, which served as our financial mainstay in two world wars, and which provide the foreign exchange we need so badly today, lies of course in our history.[26]

It has taken quite a bit of time for the United States, despite its overwhelming productive strength, to break through Britain's preferred position as the world center of finance. And, significantly, the opportunities for accomplishing this were always associated with war. At first it was the Boer War:

With England financially and economically burdened by the Boer War, a number of nations including England herself began turning to American bankers for funds. However, the cessation of the war in 1902 and the United States financial panic of 1903, interrupted this trend and dashed some premature hopes of New York's replacing London as the world's financial center.[27]

The financial pressures of the First World War opened the door much wider for a transfer of the financial center. The Allied Powers needed financing first for the arms race and then for the war itself, and much of it was found in New York. The factors underlying the drift in power from Europe to the United States were carefully evaluated by Thomas W. Lamont, the most articulate member of the firm of J. P. Morgan & Co. In an article in the July 1915 *Annals* of the American Academy of Political and Social Science, he identified the elements of the change brought about by the first year of the war and which could become increasingly important, depending on how long the war was to run: (1) "Many of our manufacturers and merchants have been doing wonderful business in articles relating to the war"; (2) the increase in war business contributed to a "prodigious export trade balance"; (3) the good export trade balance enabled buying back United States securities held by foreign investors; (4) the repurchase of these securities helped to eliminate the drain of foreign exchange that had been going to pay interest and dividends to foreigners; (5) the resulting transformation from debtor to creditor status enabled the United States to lend to foreign nations on a large scale, and thus to become a major recipient, rather than a payer, of interest and dividends.[28] But while all this was moving in the direction of a transfer of the financial center, Lamont guessed quite soberly that such changes do not come overnight:

Many people seem to believe that New York is to supersede London as the money center of the world. In order to become the money center we must of course become the trade center of the world. That is certainly a possibility. Is it a probability? Only time can show. But my guess would be that, although subsequent to the war this country is bound to be more important financially than ever before, it will be many years before America, even with her wonderful resources, energy, and success, will become the financial center of the world. Such a shifting cannot be brought about quickly, for of course to become the money center of the world we must, as I have said, become the trade center; and up to date our exports to regions other than Great Britain and Europe have been comparatively limited in amount. We must cultivate and build up new markets for our manufacturers and merchants, and all that is a matter of time.[29]

This cool and deliberate analytical ability did not interfere with Lamont's grander vision, based on deep faith that finance capital will go on forever:

When that terrible, blood-red fog of war burns away we shall see finance still standing firm. We shall see the spectacle of the business men of all nations paying to one another their just debts. We shall see the German merchant keeping his word sacred to the English; and the French to the Turk. We shall see finance standing ready to develop new enterprises; to find money to till new fields;

to help rebuild a broken and wreck-strewn world; to set the fires
of industry blazing brightly again and lighting up the earth with
the triumphs of peace.[30]

The Bolshevik repudiation of the Tsarist debts must surely
have shaken this credo. Now, finance was needed to hold back
the tide of Communism. Still, the postwar reconstruction needs
of a prostrate Europe did have its effect: it brought United
States finance into the international arena with full force. On
top of this, the flight of capital from Europe to this country
in the 20's and 30's strengthened United States finance, because
this flight occasioned an unusual accumulation of gold in the
United States. The changing tides were summarized by William
Woodruff, a historian of Europe's international role:

While there was little recognition in the immediate post-First
World War years of the essential change that had taken place, the
war had undermined Europe's position as the financial center of
the world; and without adequate finance trade could not prosper.
The Bank of England even tried to resume its nineteenth-century
role as the controlling agency in the international capital market,
and took the initiative in arranging reconstruction loans when the
war ended. Long-term lending by Britain, France, and, to a lesser
extent, by Belgium, the Netherlands, and Switzerland was renewed. Sweden also emerged as a creditor country. . . . But only
the United States possessed the financial resources needed in the
postwar period. As that country assumed some of the responsibilities of the world's greatest creditor nation there began to flow
from America to Europe a succession of loans and gifts (charity
and business have been inextricably linked) which is without parallel, and which has continued until the present day.[31]

Actually, some Marxist scholars did recognize in the early
postwar years what was impending. E. Preobrazhensky, for example, underscored in 1924 the essential nature of the new
phenomenon on the world financial scene in classic, historic-
perspective fashion:

It is interesting to recall that currency dictatorship has usually
belonged, in the course of history, to that country which played
the dominating role at any given moment in world trade and world
economy. In the period when Phoenician and Greek trade was
dominant in the Mediterranean Sea a very great role was played
by the Greek and Phoenician talent. The florin ruled in the

period when Italian merchant capital dominated the Mediterranean. The mercantile role of Spain brought the piastre to the forefront of inter-currency relations. Holland ruled not only with its fleet, its cloth, and its trade generally, but also with the gulden. As the center of gravity in world economy and trade passed to the "ruler of the waves," the British pound's role advanced to the forefront. Finally, America's economic domination of the world has led to the domination of the dollar.[32]

As is not too uncommon with analysts who take the long view, Preobrazhensky was a bit premature. The influence of the dollar, it is true, was on the rise: the result of the large increase in the export of capital from the United States and the appearance of the dollar for the first time as a reserve currency and a vehicle for international transactions. Before the First World War, other nations kept, in addition to gold, mainly British sterling (plus lesser amounts of French, Swiss, and Dutch currency) as a reserve against balance-of-payments fluctuations. The war changed that: the dollar joined sterling as a major reserve currency—but still only in a position junior to the British pound. It took still another world war, the devastation in Europe and Asia, and the financial bankruptcy of the other leading industrial powers to set the stage for the United States to take over the financial as well as military and political supremacy of the capitalist world:

Like England in its heyday, when it was the major center of world trade and finance and sterling was the key currency, the United States in turn emerged from the Second World War as the world's financial center and its currency as the most important medium of exchange.[33]

The change in the world position of the dollar since the war is quite clearly evident in the comparison of the holdings of gold versus dollars as reserves by foreign governments and their central banks (see Table XVII on the following page).

Thus, it can be seen, the dollar though accepted as an international currency before the Second World War was still a relatively small proportion of the gold reserves of central banks. Since the end of the war, however, it has assumed a major and growing significance.

To understand the import of this development, we should

TABLE XVII
GOLD AND DOLLAR HOLDINGS BY FOREIGN COUNTRIES[a]

At end of	Gold (in billions	Dollar Assets [b] of dollars)	Dollar Assets as a percent of gold
1938	$11.0	$0.5	5
1950	11.5	3.4	30
1955	14.4	7.0	49
1967	26.9	15.7	58

(a) Excludes reserves held by Communist countries. Also, excludes holdings of the International Monetary Fund.

(b) United States liquid liabilities to official institutions of foreign countries (central banks and government departments). The data prior to 1967 do not include holdings by foreign governments of U.S. government bonds and notes. These instruments were then a quite small item in the dollar assets of foreign governments. The resulting statistical discrepancy is not significant enough to affect the validity of the trend shown.

Source: *Federal Reserve Bulletin,* September 1940, December 1951, December 1956, June 1968.

first review what is meant by the dollar as a reserve currency. Money enters into the commerce of nations as payment for goods and services transferred from one country to another. When a United States manufacturer sells a refrigerator to a customer in Brazil he is paid in cruzeiros. The cruzeiro represents in effect an IOU on Brazilian goods and services: it is only useful for buying in Brazil. If, however, the United States manufacturer has nothing to buy in Brazil, he will want only United States dollars. For he can use only United States dollars to pay for the labor, raw materials and other costs of making the refrigerator, and to reap his profit. But to get paid in dollars there must be another United States businessman who needs cruzeiros. If there is such a businessman who needs cruzeiros, there can then be an exchange of cruzeiros for dollars. Obviously, only such United States businessmen will need cruzeiros as wish to buy Brazilian goods for sale in the United States (or services which are sold to United States nationals).

In the trade between nations such transactions are multiplied many times over, so that the individual needs of the importer and the exporter are accumulated through the banking system and worked out in the overall balance of international payments between nations. If the total value of exports equals the total value of imports, there is no problem about there being, for example, too many unwanted cruzeiros.[34]

However, if the exports and imports do not balance, then some means of acceptable payment has to be found by the country that has bought more than it has sold. The universally accepted means of payment, of course, is gold. Gold is the universal solvent—one that has been established over centuries, not for mythical reasons but because gold has the virtues required of a repository of value and of a generally acceptable means of payment in international exchange between "free" markets.

In recent times there have been two main exceptions to the use of gold as an international monetary reserve: the British pound and the United States dollar. This means that other countries were willing, or compelled by force of circumstances, to maintain these currencies in addition to, or as a substitute for, gold.

For the normal course of international commerce each nation must keep reserves of an acceptable means of payment, if only to smooth out the customary recurrent imbalances between exports and imports. Moreover, a country's reserve of international means of payment is the final recourse for settling bills when there is an excess of imports over exports (other than temporary adjustments funded by investments and loans by foreigners). In the final analysis, the size of a country's reserves influences the limit of how far a country can go in economic development, if its economic development depends on imports of capital goods and raw materials.

The size and viability of the reserves of international means of payments are clearly of vital import to a nation's economic well-being. When these reserves are in the form of gold, there is no present or potential restraint to the use of the reserves in any fashion a government desires. This is so because gold as a commodity has value, and is universally accepted as a means of payment.

However, when reserves consist of another nation's currency then there is a real or potential restraint. For a national currency, in the final analysis, is only good as an IOU for goods and services produced by the country issuing the currency. As long as the dollar is considered "as good as gold" by international traders and bankers, the dollar acts as a vehicle for the exchange of some 110 distinct currencies. Traders shift from one currency to another through dollars. In fact, the concept of the "as good as gold" dollar has been embodied in the very structure of the International Monetary Fund (IMF). Article IV of the treaty that established the IMF provides: "The par value of the currency of each member shall be expressed in terms of gold as a common denominator or in terms of the United States dollar of the weight and fineness in effect on July 1, 1944."

It is clear that this equating of the dollar with gold sets up a relationship of dependency of all capitalist nations on the United States. The degree of dependency will vary in accordance with the relative strength of the various capitalist nations. The reliance on the United States dollar means that in the final analysis—and this becomes painfully apparent on the brink of crisis—the holders of the United States IOU's can use them only to purchase United States goods at United States prices (assuming, of course, that the United States keeps its faith when it itself is faced with special difficulties).

As long as the leading trading nations accept the United States dollar as international money, and foreign businessmen and governments are willing to keep their reserves in United States banks, the dollar can act as a substitute for gold. This implicitly assumes that there is no end to the power and strength of the United States, and that foreign businessmen and bankers will be forever "patriots" of the United States dollar. But the underlying reality of business life is that financial ties based on interdependence can only be temporary. They last as long as there is immediate or near-term advantage—either in the form of better profits or security of one's capital. When the boat rocks, it is each man for himself. The fact that the financial power of the United States is not limitless is clearly evident in the strains already produced in domestic and international finance merely by adding the costs of the war in Vietnam on top of the costs involved in trying to hold on to United States political and military dominance throughout the capitalist world.

The key thing to understand here is the potential restraint: —the continuous danger of restraint—imposed by this involvement of the capitalist world with the dollar. The world role of the dollar has become one of the main instruments of control which the United States attempts to exercise over the capitalist world. On the one hand, the dollar as world currency is possible because of the economic and military strength of the United States. On the other hand, the very fact that the dollar has evolved as *the* international currency supplies the United States with the means to finance its activities directed towards controlling the world environment and enhancing its economic and military strength.

A sense of this role can be gathered by the way Secretary of the Treasury Henry H. Fowler moved to get the industrialized allies of this country to fall into line as this country approached an international monetary crisis in the spring of 1967. Heading a news report, "Monetary Threat Voiced by Fowler," the *New York Times* quoted him as saying:

I continue to find it necessary and relevant to emphasize to my colleagues from other countries that the way in which this nation handles its balance of payments problem depends in large measure on the cooperation it receives from other countries in the process, and upon the way in which other important financial nations act in dealing with their own domestic and international monetary problems.

I find it also necessary to emphasize that this cooperation is not a matter of helping the United States deal with its problem, but a matter of enabling the United States to deal with its problem without undermining the international monetary system, subjecting that system, by unilateral action, to radical and undesirable change, or withdrawing from commitments involving the security and development of others.[35]

Secretary Fowler's implied threat consists of two parts: (1) that the United States can by unilateral action undermine the international monetary system and thus pull the house down; and (2) the United States needs this international monetary system to carry on military action, military assistance, and economic aid—the ingredients of the United States program to preserve the imperialist world as constructed today.

Currency Blocs as Instruments of Control

In the normal course of events, the nature of the restraint imposed by the use of foreign currencies is not readily apparent: the operations of such a system are too closely interwoven with the accepted, ordinary, and taken-for-granted course of economic affairs. The uses to which such monetary arrangements can be put become crystal clear, however, when one examines their use as instruments of control by metropolitan centers over their colonies or in times of economic crisis and war.[36]

For example, one of the early measures taken by Britain, as the world depression of the 30's set in, was the development of a "sterling area" in which the members of the British Commonwealth and Empire (except Canada) participated. Included eventually were other countries which were either within the British sphere of influence or found such a defensive arrangement to their advantage. The purpose was to protect the trade of the empire and its temporary trading allies in the stiff competition of the depression onslaught. For this purpose, the "sterling area" arrangement included three features: (1) its members held sterling currency for all or part of their monetary reserve; (2) in the main, their foreign trade payments were made in sterling; and (3) the group aimed to keep their currencies stable in relation to sterling rather than to the dollar.[37]

The control potentials implicit in the use of a particular currency as a reserve became even clearer during the Second World War, when Britain was able to directly dominate the international activity of its empire through the use of Payments Agreements:

During the war Britain, seeking to live as much on credit as possible and not to engage her manpower at home on making exports merely to pay her way—save for exports urgently required to sustain the economies of countries which were furnishing her or her allies with supplies—entered into agreements, known as Payments Agreements, with most countries, whereby sterling, accruing to them by the sale to her of goods or by the provision to her of services for her forces overseas or in any other way, was to be held by them in Special Accounts and was only usable for discharge of liabilities to the sterling area.[38]

Actually, Britain went even further by requiring that the

dollar earnings of the members of the Commonwealth be spent
only with the metropolitan center's consent. Sir Dennis Robertson's caustic comment on how this dollar pool functioned is
much to the point:

It meant that each country as a country agreed to hand over
its surplus dollar earnings to Mother in exchange for sterling, and
to go to Mother when it wanted extra dollars to spend. Naturally,
the degree of confidence with which it exercised or presented
claims on the dollar pool depended partly on its political status:
the little black children who were often the best earners could be
smacked on the head if they showed too great a propensity to
spend dollars, while the grown-up white daughters, who were often
pretty extravagant, could only be quietly reasoned with.[39]

The Payments Agreements generated during the war became weapons for getting Britain back on its feet: by setting
up conditions as part of the price the colonies paid for their
independence. To this day, sterling performs a reserve function
for much of the sterling area, and acts as a medium for maintaining established trade relations against the erosion introduced by the competition of the United States and other countries. France, too, still uses the franc as the trading and reserve
medium for many of the present or former French overseas territories.

But it is not only in times of austerity or when there is an
established colonial tie that the reserve currency role acts as
a lever for influence and control. Along with the United States
take-over of the military responsibility of the capitalist nations in
the Pacific, the economic influence over even British Commonwealth nations in that area also grows. What is happening in
Australia is a useful illustration. As the flow of United States
capital to Australia rises (almost half of Australia's capital inflow now comes from the United States) and trade with the
United States swells, the policy issue confronting Australia is
whether or not to shift from the sterling to the dollar sphere
of influence, and accordingly to decide which currency to use
for reserve purposes. An *Economist* (London) report comments:

The proportion of the reserves held [by Australia] in sterling
has now slumped to 60 percent, from 80 percent as recently as 1960
and from all of 94 percent at the beginning of the 1950's.

Top Australians, who make the decisions about these matters, are absolutely firm about asserting Australia's loyalty to the sterling area. But public discussion about the merits of staying with sterling is no longer thought treasonable, and there has been some debate about it this year in the Australian financial press. One widely held unofficial view is that Australia might secure privileged access to the American capital market, like Canada and Japan, if it switched to the American dollar bloc. Another view is that it might be worth staying with sterling—if Britain manages to get into the Common Market.

Given the big swing that has already taken place in Australian trade and overseas borrowing it is hardly surprising that the dollar content of Australia's reserves has risen twelve-fold over the past 17 years and three-fold since 1960.[40]

The Devaluation Road

The economic advantage accruing to a country by its involvement in international banking and the use of its currency as a reserve currency is also revealed in the different roads of adjustment taken by the leading industrial powers and the economically dependent nations when imbalances crop up in international payments transactions.

Normally when a country faces a deficit in its international account—i.e. when it has to pay out more than it receives—it has recourse either to its reserves of gold and foreign currency or to borrowing from foreign bankers (or government institutions). Once these means are exhausted, a deficit country must face an internal adjustment process which reduces itself mainly to a reduction of purchases from abroad. To a lesser extent the problem is attacked by trying to expand exports— lesser because a country can more easily control imports than expand exports, especially when increasing exports often means trying to get more sales in the very moribund markets which helped create the imbalance in the first place.

Reduction in imports can sometimes be achieved by higher tariffs or by direct controls. This itself can induce a slump owing to the impact of a reduction in the import of raw materials and intermediate products. A more effective technique for a "free enterprise" economy is to take measures that will more directly induce a slump, as, for example, lowering wages to reduce consumption or restricting credit to damp down production. An economic decline will cut the demand for imports and help remove the deficit.

In most cases a persistent and severe deficit ultimately induces devaluation. Countries are inclined to take this measure only as a last resort because of the enormous dislocations usually induced thereby. Devaluation brings about a rigorously enforced adjustment through the market place: it raises the prices of imported goods, thus forcing a reduction in consumption, especially by those social classes with low incomes; it reduces the prices of exports in foreign markets, thus putting exported goods in a more competitive position.

It is especially noteworthy, in the context of the present discussion, that recourse to either severe internal adjustments or 'devaluation is a common feature of the economically and financially dependent nations and is much less frequent in the centers of financial power. This was so even in what economists consider the heyday of a smoothly working international system. The gold standard of the 19th century was supposed to have been an ideal market mechanism for keeping international finance on an even keel. But automatic mechanisms are more often the product of the abstractions and models created by the thought processes of economists than a representation of reality. The fact is that the so-called automatic gold standard operated through the channels of the international money market centers. The adjustments called for by the gold standard were made through the credit operations of the international bankers and the international transfers of capital made by these bankers. It is little wonder then that these operations worked to induce exchange-rate stability in the advanced countries and instability in the countries of the "periphery." In a summary analysis of the gold standard mechanism, the first two observations made by Professor Robert Triffin are:

(1) The nineteenth-century monetary mechanism succeeded, to a unique degree, in preserving exchange-rate stability—and freedom from quantitative trade and exchange restrictions—over a large part of the world.

(2) *The success, however, was limited to the more advanced countries which formed the core of the system, and to those closely*

linked to them by political, as well as economic and financial ties. The exchange rates of other currencies—particularly in Latin America—fluctuated widely, and depreciated enormously, over the period. The contrast between the "core" countries and those of the "periphery" can be largely explained by the *cyclical pattern of capital movements and terms of trade, which contributed to stability in the first group, and to instability in the second.*[41] (Emphasis added.)

The point is that the main banking centers had the power and the mechanisms made available by this power to smooth out deficit problems, in contrast with the dependent countries in the capitalist world system, where financial discipline was imposed by the undiluted pressures of the market. In another context, Triffin observes:

The second factor which explains the successful functioning of nineteenth century convertibility lies in the fact that the emergence of *major* imbalance was *prevented ex ante* by the institutional monetary and banking framework of the times, rather than *corrected ex post* by large price and income adjustments. In spite of the greater flexibility of prices and costs in the nineteenth century, I doubt very much whether a 20 or 30 percent reduction in wages, if called for to restore equilibrium in the balance of payments, would have been tolerated then any more than it would be today. The fact is that the ability of the system to correct such major maladjustments through internal price and income adaptations was rarely put to a test in the major Western countries which constituted the core of the system. Whenever it was put to such a test—as it repeatedly was in most Latin American countries—the correction was uniformly brought about by currency devaluation. . . .[42]

In effect, the persistent devaluations of the underdeveloped countries result in repeated adjustments of the *internal* price structure of these countries to the *external* price structure of world trade.[43] The latter is one that evolved in a fashion best suited to establish and strengthen the supremacy of the leading world traders—the same countries that are the leading financial centers. The process of devaluation is a process of bringing the prices of the weaker nations into line with those of the stronger nations.

The differences in the path of adjustment of internal to world prices are to be seen in the 20th century as well as in the

19th. Even in the face of war-caused devastation and economic distortions in leading industrial and financial centers, the differences in the degree and impact of devaluation are noteworthy. The contrast for different regions since 1948 is shown in the following table, from a study by Margaret de Vries, consultant to the IMF:

TABLE XVIII
EXTENT OF DEVALUATION
1948 TO 1967

Region	Number of Countries	Average Weighted Devaluation (Percent)
Australia, Canada, New Zealand, and the United States	4	5.2
Europe	20	23.5
Middle East	12	38.4
Asia (excluding Japan)	14	46.1
Africa	36	47.6
Latin America	23	62.2

Source: Margaret G. de Vries, "The Magnitudes of Exchange Devaluations," *Finance and Development*, No. 2, 1968, p. 10.

The differences in the degree of devaluation are influenced, it would seem, by the relative degree of financial dependency. Among the underdeveloped countries, two patterns are visible. A number of them are so closely intertwined with a particular industrialized country that their devaluations follow that of the major currencies: in the process of currency adjustment, these countries follow the lead of the "mother" country. Thus, many nations in Asia and Africa devalued in proportions similar to the British pound or the French franc. In those underdeveloped countries where the economic and financial dependency are enforced to a greater extent by the market place, the extent of devaluation has been much more substantial. For these supposedly more independent countries, devaluations of from 40 to nearly 100 percent were experienced during this period from 1948 to 1967.

It is sometimes argued that the greater devaluations characteristic of Latin American countries are due to their special propensity for inflation. The de Vries study shows, however, that in the unusually inflationary countries, the extent of currency depreciation in real terms has been greater than the inflation itself would induce.[44]

Contrasts in Devaluation Experience

Why is it, then, that the major centers of financial power have fewer and less severe balance of payments problems than do the underdeveloped countries? And why, when they do have such problems, are the devaluations and internal economic adjustments (economic slumps, sharp reductions in consumption) rarer and less austere?

The answer to these questions cannot be fully explored within the limits of this presentation. But, in summary form, the reasons can be traced to three differences between the major economic powers and the satellites of these powers: (1) industrial structure, (2) world trade relations, and (3) degree of financial strength (or independence).

An industrialized nation has the distinct advantage of flexibility of resources: it can create its own means of production; it can produce its own machine tools and other capital equipment; it has the experienced engineering and labor supply; it usually has stockpiles of raw materials, if only in the pipelines of production and trade. The best example of this flexibility is the speed and efficiency with which these nations turn from production for peace to production for war and back again. With this flexibility an industrial power can more readily adapt its production to changes in demand on the world market. In the first place, an industrialized nation is not dependent for its income from abroad on the exports of only one or two products; hence a drop in market demand for one group of products has only limited effect on the balance of payments (except of course in times of world-wide depression, when the decline in exports is likely to cover the whole range of goods in foreign trade). In the second place, an industrialized nation can shift relatively quickly to new products and new styles to take advantage of new types of demand. A classic illustration of this is the success of Japanese industry and export trade in the postwar years (helped along, to be sure, by United States cooperation to create a junior bastion in the Pacific, and by the stimulation afforded by United States purchases for the Korean and Vietnamese wars).

The industrial and financial centers have still a further advantage: they are much less dependent than the under-developed countries on exports of material goods for their foreign exchange. The financial centers have a source of income in the very financial services (such as insurance and banking) that they provide. In addition, their large merchant fleets get a good share of income from moving overseas merchandise. And the real whipped cream topping is the inflow of interest and profits from overseas investments and loans. Thus, between 30 and 35 percent of the foreign exchange earnings from goods and services of the United States and the United Kingdom arises from services, including the income from investment and loans; the remaining 65 to 70 percent comes from the sale of commodities. In contrast, the typical case in the underdeveloped countries (except for countries like Mexico that get consider-able tourist income) is for 90 to 95 percent of the foreign ex-change arising from the sale of goods and services to come from export of goods.

The advantageous maneuverability of the industrial na-tions highlights the handicaps of the underdeveloped countries. For, in the main, the productive capacity of the latter has been created or transformed by foreign capital to conform to the needs of the investors of capital. Their industrial (and agri-cultural and mining) structure is inflexible and confined primarily to meeting the specific demands of the major in-dustrial powers for food, fuel, minerals, and other raw materials. An inspection of Table XIX will demonstrate this point. First, there is the sharp differentiation between the extractive and non-extractive industries: less than a third of the exports from the developed countries comes from the extractive industries, while over four fifths of the exports from the underdeveloped countries are of this type. Second, even the relatively small percentage of non-extractive exports from the underdeveloped world are in the "other manufactured goods" class—consisting mainly of light industry and handicrafts.

TABLE XIX

THE PATTERNS OF EXPORT TRADE
(1960-1965 ANNUAL AVERAGES)

	EXPORTS FROM			
	Developed Countries		Underdeveloped Countries	
Class of Products	Billions of Dollars	Percent of total	Billions of Dollars	Percent of total
Extractive Industries	$29.2	30.0	$24.3	83.8
Food, Beverages & Tobacco	13.9	14.3	8.4	28.9
Crude Materials, excluding mineral fuels	11.6	11.9	6.8	23.5
Mineral Fuels	3.7	3.8	9.1	31.4
Non-extractive Industries	68.0	70.0	4.7	16.2
Chemicals	7.7	8.0	0.4	1.3
Machinery and Transport Equipment	28.5	29.3	0.3	0.9
Other Manufactured Goods	30.6	31.5	3.9	13.6
Miscellaneous	1.2	1.2	0.1	0.4
Total	$97.1	100.0	$29.0	100.0

Note: Developed countries: United States, Canada, West Europe, Australia, New Zealand, South Africa, and Japan.
Underdeveloped countries: all countries other than developed and Communist countries.

Source: United Nations, *Statistical Yearbook 1966,* New York, 1967.

As a rule, the bulk of the foreign exchange income of the underdeveloped countries comes from one to four natural-resource products. This can be seen from the list of principal exports given in Table XX. A reduction in world demand for any one product is almost sure to trigger a balance-of-payments emergency. Their balance-of-payments condition is also constantly influenced by the need to devote a significant portion of their exports to pay for the privilege of having foreign capital: profits, interest, and amortization of loans. When exports decline, most of these payments still have to be made: hence, the more critical the balance-of-payments emergencies.

Since the lines of world trade are limited for these satellite nations and since their economies are rigidly adapted to meeting just these lines of trade, their recourse in emergencies is to borrow foreign currency from foreign banks or governments to stave off bankruptcy. Banks, on the other hand, are not institutions of charity. If they are to stay in business and make a profit they have to make sound loans—loans backed by reliable collateral and with assurance that the loan and the interest on the loan can be repaid. Moreover, they want to be repaid in the same currency in which the loan was made. The protective provisions in loan contracts are not confined to private banking; the same considerations underlie loans made to under-developed nations by international institutions, such as the IMF and World Bank.

The underlying ties of the periphery countries as debtors to the financial centers is somewhat analogous to the perpetual economic dependency of the peasant on the landlord or money lender. The very conditions which produce the necessity to borrow money are continuously reimposed by the pressures to pay back the loan and to pay the interest on these loans. The ability of the "agricultural" countries—the producers of food and raw materials for the advanced nations—to repay their loans and interest within a limited period rests on continuing to produce the goods proven to be acceptable in world trade. And foreign currency for servicing the loans can only be attained in the short run by these same exports. Moreover, a significant part of the surplus product which might otherwise be used to diversify their economies and increase their productivity must be appropriated for debt servicing as well as paying the profits of foreign investment.

Thus, the conditions that contribute to balance-of-payments crises are reinforced by the financial means which are available for alleviating the crisis. The dependency on particular lines of world trade and the rigidity of resources to meet the special needs of the industrialized nations are repeatedly re-established with every new emergency induced by this dependency. To the extent that breaking out of this mold requires an economic and social revolution, it is not reasonable to look to bankers to finance the revolution.

TABLE XX

LEADING EXPORT COMMODITIES OF UNDERDEVELOPED NATIONS (BASED ON 1967 TRADE DATA)

Country	Number of Leading Export Commodities	Export of Leading Commodities As Percent of Total Exports	Leading Export Commodities
Argentina	4	61	Meat, Wheat, Corn, Wool
Bolivia	1	63	Tin
Brazil	4	58	Coffee, Iron Ore, Cotton, Cocoa
Cameroon*	3	65	Cocoa, Coffee, Aluminum
Central African Republic	3	90	Diamonds, Coffee, Cotton
Ceylon	3	89	Tea, Rubber, Coconut
Chile	3	85	Copper, Iron Ore, Nitrates
Colombia	2	69	Coffee, Oil
Congo, Democ. Republic*	4	74	Copper, Tin, Diamonds, Coffee
Congo (Brazzaville)	2	76	Wood, Diamonds
Costa Rica*	2	60	Coffee, Bananas
Dominican Republic	5	91	Sugar, Coffee, Cocoa, Bauxite, Tobacco
Ecuador*	3	84	Bananas, Coffee, Cocoa
Ethiopia	4	84	Coffee, Hides and Skins, Cereals, Oil seeds

Country	Number of Leading Export Commodities	Export of Leading Commodities As Percent of Total Exports	Leading Export Commodities
Gabon	4	86	Wood, Manganese, Oil, Uranium
Ghana	4	78	Cocoa, Diamonds, Wood, Manganese
Guatemala*	4	69	Coffee, Cotton, Bananas, Sugar
Guyana	4	83	Sugar, Bauxite, Alumina, Rice
Haiti*	3	68	Coffee, Sugar, Sisal
Honduras*	3	67	Bananas, Coffee, Wood
Iran	1	91	Oil
Iraq	1	92	Oil
Ivory Coast	3	81	Coffee, Cocoa, Wood
Jamaica*	4	75	Alumina, Bauxite, Sugar, Bananas
Libya	1	99	Oil
Malaysia	4	73	Rubber, Tin, Wood, Iron Ore
Mauritania*	1	91	Iron Ore
Nicaragua	5	69	Cotton, Coffee, Meat, Cottonseed, Sugar
Nigeria	3	69	Oil, Peanuts, Coffee
Paraguay	6	77	Meat, Wood, Cotton, Quebracho, Tobacco, Oil seeds
Peru	6	78	Copper, Fishmeal, Cotton, Silver, Lead, Sugar
Philippines	3	70	Coconut, Sugar, Wood
Sierra Leone*	3	78	Diamonds, Iron Ore, Palm Kernels
Uganda*	3	83	Coffee, Cotton, Rubber
Uruguay	3	84	Wool, Meat, Hides
Venezuela	2	98	Oil, Iron Ore
Vietnam, South	2	90	Rubber, Rice

---

* Data for 1966 or latest year for which reports are available.

Note: Since these data are based on one year's experience, they should not be used as a final description for any one country. In any one year, the composition of products may shift due to market conditions or internal production difficulties. The purpose of this tabulation is to show the general pattern of dependency on a limited number of products going into the export trade.

Source: Calculated from International Monetary Fund, *International Financial Statistics*, July 1968.

Financial Centers Create Their Own Money

The focal point of the network of economic relations between the great industrial powers and between these powers and the rest of the imperialist world is found in the concentrated financial power of the international money markets. As remarked earlier, the headquarters of the capitalist system is the money market. The financial power exercised through the banks and other institutions of the money market enables the industrialized nations to fend off or alleviate balance-of-payments difficulties; it is also the power which, directly or indirectly, keeps the underdeveloped countries in line as the raw materials suppliers. This does not happen as a plot or conspiracy; it results from the normal and self-defense behavior of capital.

The source of financial power, in its crudest form, is the ability to create and use money as a means of exchange and a means of payment. The creation of money used to pay for investments and to make loans arises in two banking activities: (a) the conversion of inactive into active funds, and (b) the creation of credit. The creation of money through the extension of credit (or the printing of money) is at the heart of modern banking.[45] The Brazilian bank and the Chilean bank are able to do this too. But who, outside of Brazil, other than importers of Brazilian products, wants cruzeiros? And who outside Chile, other than importers of Chilean products, wants escudos? The predicament for such countries is that they have too much of their own currency and not enough foreign currency.

Quite the reverse is the situation with respect to the diversified and large world traders in desired manufactured goods. Their money is useful internationally for several reasons: (1) It can be used for the settlement of debts, even between other foreign countries. In normal circumstances, Belgian money can be converted into French, French into British, British into United States, etc. (2) These countries produce a multitude of products wanted by the underdeveloped countries and by other industrial nations. In other words, their IOU's are usable. (3) Through colonial and sphere-of-influence arrangements, the underdeveloped countries are typically lined up in special trading channels with one or more of the major nations. Because of these trading blocs, former French territories will be able to settle balance-of-payments deficits with French francs, because a good part, if not all, of their debt outstanding is to French firms. The same is true for the spheres-of-influence of British and other financial centers.

These, then, are the reasons why the ability to create money (or, expand the money supply) by the leading industrial and financial powers is of use not only to their domestic economy but to their international economic relations as well. Because of this ability, they can (1) finance a deficit they themselves may have with a satellite nation, and (2) extend loans to satellite nations when the latter have deficits, and in the process keep them close to mother's skirts. Moreover, they can frequently ward off impending deficits in their own balance-of-payments with the rest of the world. This is done by internal credit controls, changes in interest rates, and other maneuvers by which, for example, needed capital (foreign currency or gold) can be attracted for a time from another financial center (the money market of another industrial and financial power).

The technical ins and outs of these operations cannot be spelled out here. Suffice it to say that it is through this very financial power, and the banking mechanisms through which this power is exercised, that the advanced capitalist nations are able to cope with balance-of-payments fluctuations without drastic damage to their economy; indeed, under proper conditions, they are valuable instruments for economic growth and development.

Naturally, there are limits to the creation of credit for domestic and international operations, limits that are rooted in the nature of the underlying productive capacity and the uses to which this capacity is put. When these limits are reached, whether as a result of war or preparation for war or too rapid accumulation of capital, or trying to bite off more than the country can digest, crises of various degrees set in. But even these crises are of a different order than those of the satellites. For the latter, the issue is one of survival as a dependency of a metropolitan center, under which the ruling elite can remain in power. For the metropolitan centers, the issue posed by financial crises is usually how to jockey for position with respect to other financial centers and how to maintain their existing empires: for example, Britain striving from one devaluation to another to maintain the sterling bloc, its worldwide military and naval bases, and the remnants of colonial relationships.

The Case of United States Finance

The most extravagant and unparalleled use of financial power for control over other parts of the world is that exercised by the United States since the Second World War. In every year since 1950, with the exception of a single year during the Suez Crisis, the United States balance-of-payments has been in deficit. Three main points should be fully and clearly understood in considering this persistent deficit.

(1) The deficit has been created and maintained only as part and parcel of the United States role as organizer and leader of the imperialist system. This can be seen by a quick survey of the 1967 balance-of-payments, as shown in Table XXI, the 1967 pattern being similar to that of the entire preceding era of deficits.

TABLE XXI
U.S. BALANCE OF PAYMENTS SUMMARY: 1967
(BILLIONS OF DOLLARS)

Purpose	Money Received From Abroad	Money Going Abroad
Balance on exports and imports of goods and services	+$7.9	
Private and Government remittances [a]		− $1.2
Military expenditures, net		− 3.1
Military assistance and economic aid		− 4.0
Private capital investment		− 3.5
Total	+$7.9	−$11.8

(a) Gifts sent abroad by United States nationals; payments by the government to individuals abroad, such as social security payments to persons living abroad.

Source: *Survey of Current Business,* June 1968.

The facts are as simple as they can be. The deficit is used to finance:

• Military expenditures—for the war in Vietnam and to maintain air, naval, and infantry forces over a large section of the globe. (This does not, of course, include all such expenditures, only that part which results in transferring dollars abroad.)
• Military assistance and economic aid: the instruments used for exercising United States control over other nations.
• Investment by United States industry and finance in foreign countries.

(2) The deficit is financed by the expansion of the supply of United States dollars via the credit created by the government and by banks. Professor James Tobin, former member of the President's Council of Economic Advisors, testified in 1963 before a Congressional committee as follows:

Under the reserve currency system properly functioning, the initial beneficiary of an increase in the supply of international money is obviously the reserve currency itself. It is pleasant to have a mint or printing press in one's backyard, and the gold exchange standard gave us, no less than South Africa, this privilege. We were able to run deficits in our balance of payments for 10 years because our IOU's were generally acceptable as money.[46]

(3) We can finance the deficit over so long a period because the United States is the world banker and the rest of the capitalist world has been willing (though chafing at the bit, lately) to hold dollars as a reserve asset.

The case was clearly summarized by the then Secretary of the Treasury C. Douglas Dillon, when asked by Senator Javits what benefits the United States obtains from being the world's banker. Mr. Dillon declared that

we have a very real benefit in that we have been allowed to finance our deficits through increased foreign holdings of dollars. If we had not been a reserve currency, if we had not been a world banker, this would not have happened. It would have been the same situation as other countries face; as soon as we got into deficit we would have had to balance our accounts one way or another even though it meant restricting imports, as Canada had to do last year, or cutting back our military expenditures much more drastically than our security would warrant. . . . I would say that is the chief area of benefit although there is one other very important one and that is that somebody had to be the world banker and provide this extra international liquidity. It has been the United States, which is proper, because we are the most powerful financial country and we had the most powerful currency.[47]

The former Under Secretary of the Treasury for Monetary Affairs adds another reason for the cooperation of other countries, in addition to the financial power of the United States:

Moreover, the political stability and enormous economic and military strength of the United States have also increased the desirability of keeping balances here rather than in any other country in the world.[48]

Of course, any other country in the world that tried handling as big a deficit as that of the United States for even a few years, let alone 18 years, would be in for a major depression along with a drastic reduction in the country's living standards. But then no other country would incur such deficits for such noble purposes.

Witness the exchange between Senator Proxmire and Under Secretary of the Treasury Roosa at a Congressional hearing:

Senator Proxmire. If we had no domestic considerations, if we were not also burdened with world leadership as the world banker, the classic, ideal and still effective way to bring about balance in our international payments would be an austerity program, I presume.

Secretary Roosa. Yes.

Senator Proxmire. In other words, a program that would be deflationary?

Secretary Roosa. Yes.

Senator Proxmire. Drive our prices down so that we can sell abroad, drive our wages down, reduce federal spending sharply?

Secretary Roosa. Yes.

Senator Proxmire. Increase taxes, hike interest rates, and so forth?

Secretary Roosa. Yes.

Senator Proxmire. Obviously we can do none of these things because that would be disastrous domestically and that would also contribute to an international depression?

Secretary Roosa. Yes.[49]

This exchange followed upon Under Secretary Roosa's presentation in a formal statement, which summarizes the case in more orderly fashion. If we had not been a world banker, he said,

we might have been forced long ago to cut down our imports (perhaps through deflation of our economy), reduce materially our foreign investments, income from which make a substantial contribution to our current balance of payments, and curtail, perhaps sharply, our military and economic assistance to our friends and allies. Had we taken these steps, our customers abroad would have sharply reduced their purchases in this country and we would now be confronted with discriminatory policies against the dollar in most countries of the world. Instead of the rapid growth of world trade, we would have witnessed stagnation that would have been harmful to our own prosperity and to that of the whole free world.[50]

Here then is the synthesis of today's imperialist network of international relations. The United States as leader has the economic power to invade the industry and markets of its chief trading partners and politico-military allies. It has the resources to maintain a dominant world military position. It can carry on foreign aid, invest in and lend to the underdeveloped countries, thus tying them closer to the United States through the resulting financial dependency of these countries. All of this, plus the maintenance of prosperity and fending off depressions, is made feasible because of the position of the United States as the world banker and of the dollar as the world reserve currency. And it can be the world banker and supply the reserve currency, because of the cooperation its military and economic strength commands among the other industrialized nations. And, necessarily, within the United States this is accompanied by "an inexorable entanglement of private business with foreign policy."[51]

The cooperation of the other industrial nations is not the fruit of pure wisdom. It came at a time when these countries had little choice. Roosa's comment on this is noteworthy:

The dollar reached its pre-eminent position, of course, during and immediately following World War II when there was in reality no other currency available to play a world role and when so much of our governmental assistance was made available in freely usable dollars. By the time some of the European countries achieved convertibility and large surpluses, the dollar was deeply entrenched in the usages of trade and payments throughout the world. . . . And so long as the American economy remains committed to principles of market freedom, there will be American banks and other financial institutions here eagerly seeking to perform the banking functions identified with the dollar's role as the vehicle currency. From that role, in my view, we cannot in practice withdraw, short of a revolutionary change in our entire economic structure.[52]

The central bankers of the other imperialist centers are as well aware as Mr. Roosa, now a partner of Brown Brothers Harriman and Company, of the "revolutionary" implications to the United States economic structure and consequently to the rest of the capitalist world of a basic departure from the present international monetary system. What is at stake here is not mere adjustments in the credit mechanism of the International Monetary Fund—the kind of monetary reforms now being introduced and considered—but the central issue of the dollar as the international currency. At the same time, the partners of the United States in this monetary system have their own necks to protect and their own competitive interests to pursue. The source of fear of the central bankers of other nations is traceable to the ordinary common sense of international banking, and is simply summarized in the data shown in Table XXII.

What this table shows is the simultaneous movement in opposite directions of gold reserves and dollar obligations to foreigners: the rapid decline of United States gold reserves and accumulation of dollar holdings by foreigners. At the end of May 1968, the liquid dollar assets held by foreigners were almost three times the gold held by the United States. In case of a "run on the bank"—if all foreigners who own dollars should over a short period ask the United States to make good on its paper IOUs, the United States would be some $20 billion short of the universally acceptable means of payment, gold.

The magnitude of the difference between gold reserves and dollar obligations to foreigners is an important indicator of the financial limits of U.S. external activities. That such limits exist was made more apparent as the United States balance-of-payments deficits kept mounting from year to year, despite the opposition of other money centers: the arrogance

TABLE XXII

U.S. GOLD RESERVES VS. DOLLAR LIABILITIES TO FOREIGNERS (BILLIONS OF DOLLARS)

End of	Gold Reserves of the United States	Dollar Assets Held by Foreigners [a]
1955	21.8	11.7
1960	17.8	18.7
May 1968	10.7	31.5

(a) The 1960 and 1968 data are liquid liabilities of the United States to other governments and to foreign banks and other foreign institutions and businessmen. The 1955 data are short-term liabilities and do not include United States government bonds held by foreigners. This lack of comparability does not negate the point made here; a comparable figure for 1955 would probably be somewhat higher than $11.7 billion, but not by more than 10 percent. Note that the data on dollar holdings are considerably in excess of those shown in Table XVII. The latter include only dollar holdings of foreign governments and their central banks. The data shown here are the total liquid dollar obligations to foreigners, including banks, other financial institutions and businessmen.

Source: United States Bureau of the Census, *Statistical Abstract 1966*, Washington, D.C., 1967 and *Federal Reserve Bulletin*, August 1968.

of United States foreign military and economic operations was matched by the arrogance of its international financial practice. Shaken from time to time by gold and currency speculators on European exchanges, the United States continues its financial practices, with increasing limitations, by relying ultimately on the voluntary and involuntary cooperation of the central bankers of other nations.

Most of the nations in the imperialist network have no alternative: as creditors of the United States government and banks they must submit to being members of what is virtually the dollar bloc. The more independent metropolitan centers, however, do have some options. Almost half of the dollar obligations to foreigners are concentrated in six nations: Britain, Japan, France, West Germany, Italy, and Switzerland. They therefore have the weapons with which to pressure the United States. Nevertheless, under present circumstances, their options are limited. Their interests are aligned with the United States to the extent that United States military and economic power is used to secure the imperialist system and push back, if possible, the borders of the non-imperialist world. At the same time they are worried about their own skin and the competitive threat of United States business and finance. Hence, the jockeying for power that does take place operates within the limits of present international monetary arrangements. It is important always to keep in mind that at the heart of the conflicts of international finance is a struggle over *power*. This was well pointed out by Eugene A. Birnbaum, senior economist for Standard Oil Company (New Jersey):

We may ask why, after a hundred years of internal monetary conferences, men still have not resolved their differences. The answer lies in one word—*power*. That is what one hundred years of international monetary conferences have been about. The 22nd meeting of the International Monetary Fund held at Rio, where a new facility for creating international liquidity was recommended, is no exception to this general rule.[53]

Maneuvers over reforms in the international money system are only one form of the power struggle. The tensions within the centers of imperialist power show up in many ways. Within the dominant business circles of the other industrial powers are groups whose immediate business interests are tied up with those of the United States, while others see their profit opportunities shrinking in the face of United States expansion. Both as a self-defense measure against United States expansion and because of the inner dynamics of their own economies, foreign business firms and banks are engaging in their own outward expansion via export of capital, international banking, and the use of economic and military aid by their governments in underdeveloped nations.

At work are three main vectors: (1) centripetal forces binding the main financial centers with the United States for the preservation of the imperialist network; (2) centrifugal forces, stimulated by profit competition, seeking special advantages as weak spots in United States operations show up; and (3) "vertical cohesion," with each imperialist center trying to consolidate the economic and financial ties with their colonial and sphere-of-influence areas. It is in this last context that foreign aid as a technique of control over the underdeveloped nations has caught hold and become increasingly strategic.

NOTES

1. Jeremy Main, "The First Real International Bankers," *Fortune,* December 1967, p. 143.
2. T. M. Farley, *The "Edge Act" and United States International Banking and Finance,* New York, Brown Brothers Harriman & Co., May 1962, p. 32.
3. *New York Times,* December 9, 1965.
4. *Business Week,* October 14, 1967, p. 92.
5. Dr. Christoph Beringer and Irshad Ahmad, *The Use of Agricultural Surplus Commodities for Economic Development in Pakistan,* Karachi, January 1964, p. 14.
6. George S. Moore, "International Growth: Challenge to U.S. Banks," *The National Banking Review,* September 1963, p. 6.
7. Herbert Feis, *Europe The World's Banker, 1870-1914,* New York, 1965, pp. 30-31.
8. Frank M. Tamagna and Parker B. Willis, "United States Banking Organization Abroad," *Federal Reserve Bulletin,* December 1965, p. 1287.
9. William Adams Brown, Jr., *The International Gold Standard Reinterpreted,* 1914-34, New York, 1940, Vol. I, pp. 147-148.
10. William S. Kies, "Branch Banks and our Foreign Trade," in The American Academy of Political and Social Science, *The Annals,* May 1915, p. 301.
11. *Ibid.,* p. 308.
12. *Ibid.,* p. 307.
13. Calculated from mimeographed list issued by the Federal Reserve Board, *Overseas Branches and Corporations Engaged in Foreign Banking and Financing in Operation on December 31, 1967.*
14. Is there perhaps an affinity between United States branch banking abroad and social revolution? In 1917, the largest concentration of United States branch banks in any one foreign country was in Russia. Prior to the Chinese revolution, the largest concentration of United States branch banks in the Far East was in China. And Cuba was also a long-time favorite for United States banking: prior to the Cuban revolution, Cuba was host to the largest number of United States bank branches.

15. Jeremy Main, *op. cit.*, p. 143.
16. Charles B. Kindleberger, "European Economic Integration and the Development of a Single Financial Center for Long-Term Capital," *Weltwirtschaftliches Archiv,* Bd. 90, Heft 2, 1963, p. 206. As in the case of United States manufacturing industry in Europe, the growing influence of United States banking on the continent and in England is stimulating countermoves in the form of mergers. It is generally recognized that the steps taken to merge Barclays, Lloyds, and Martins, leading banks of England, were largely designed to cope with the increased competition of United States banks in England and in the customary overseas areas of British banking.
17. Hugh Chairnoff, "Philadelphia Bankers are International Bankers," Federal Reserve Bank of Philadelphia *Business Review,* May 1968, pp. 2-3. Another interesting contributing factor is the ability of large banks outside the Eastern centers of the country to capture banking business in the more rapidly growing areas of the United States. Other than the Bank of America, it is the Eastern banks that are most involved in foreign business and are in the best position to seek further business abroad.
18. Jeremy Main, *op cit.*, pp. 143-144.
19. Same as footnote 13.
20. T. M. Farley, *op cit.*, p. 27.
21. Neil McInness, "The Continental Touch," *Barron's,* November 28, 1966.
22. For examples of these types of loans, see T. M. Farley, *op cit.*, pp. 43-45.
23. *Ibid.*, p. 43.
24. David Rockefeller, *Economic Development: The Banking Aspects,* The Per Jacobsson Memorial Lecture at the International Monetary Fund Meeting, Rio de Janeiro, September 22, 1967, The Chase Manhattan Bank, p. 14.
25. Thomas Balogh, *Unequal Partners,* Oxford, England, 1963, Vol. II, p. 25.
26. Lord Comer, Speech at Guildhall, Bank of England *Quarterly Bulletin,* March 1966, pp. 51-52.
27. T. M. Farley, *op cit.*, p. 5.
28. Thomas W. Lamont, "The Effect of the War on America's Financial Position," in The American Academy of Political and Social Science, *The Annals,* July 1915, pp. 106-112.
29. *Ibid.*, pp. 108-109.
30. *Ibid.*, p. 112.
31. William Woodruff, *Impact of Western Man, A Study of Europe's Role in the World Economy 1750-1960,* London, 1966, p. 277.
32. E. Preobrazhensky, *The New Economics,* Oxford, England, 1965, p. 155. This book merits more attention by students. For the subject discussed here, see the entire section, pp. 150-160.
33. Henry G. Aubrey, *The Dollar in World Affairs, An Essay in International Financial Policy,* New York, 1964, p. 109.
34. In this simplified explanation, we are ignoring capital movements. While the balance of payments problem cannot be properly analyzed without taking capital movements into account, the main issues can

be explained for the present purpose by referring merely to the balance of goods and services.

35. *New York Times,* March 18, 1967.

36. For a description of the British practice in keeping control over its colonies, both before and after independence, as applied to Ghana, see Bob Fitch and Mary Oppenheimer, *Ghana: End of an Illusion,* New York, Monthly Review Press, 1966, pp. 42-47. For a more general treatment applied to African nations, before and after independence, see Thomas Balogh, *The Economics of Poverty,* London, 1966, Chapter 2, "The Mechanism of Neo-Imperialism."

37. R. F. Harrod, *The Pound Sterling,* Princeton Essays in International Finance, No. 13, Princeton, February 1952, p. 9.

38. R. F. Harrod, *International Economics,* Cambridge, England, 1957, pp. 99-100.

39. Sir Dennis Robertson, *Britain in the World Economy,* London, 1954, p. 39, as quoted in Fitch and Oppenheimer, *op. cit.,* p. 46. A significant sidelight on this question became manifest when the United States, the richest and most powerful country, insisted on the elimination of the trade competition involved in the "sterling area" and the "dollar pool" as a condition for giving financial aid to war devastated Britain. Article 7 of the Financial Agreement Between the Government of the United States and the United Kingdom, December 6, 1945, reads: "The Government of the United Kingdom will complete arrangements as early as practicable and in any case not later than one year after the effective date of this Agreement . . . under which . . . the sterling receipts from current transactions of all sterling area countries . . . will be freely available for current transactions in any currency area without discrimination; with the result that any discrimination arising from the so-called sterling area dollar pool will be entirely removed and that each member of the sterling area will have its current sterling and dollar receipts at its free disposition for current transactions anywhere." (The Agreement is reprinted as an appendix to Richard N. Gardner, *Sterling-Dollar Diplomacy,* Oxford, England, 1956.)

40. *The Economist,* October 7, 1967, p. 89.

41. Robert Triffin, *The Evolution of the International Monetary System: Historical Reappraisal and Future Perspectives* (Princeton Studies in International Finance No. 12), Princeton, New Jersey, 1964, p. 9.

42. Robert Triffin, *Gold and the Dollar Crisis,* New Haven, 1961, p. 27.

43. For a suggestive comment on the tension between internal and external prices, see Nicholas Kaldor, "International Trade and Economic Development," *Problems of Foreign Aid* (Report of a Conference at The University College, November 1964), Dar es Salaam, Tanzania, 1965, pp. 82-85.

44. Margaret G. de Vries, "The Magnitudes of Exchange Devaluation," *Finance and Development,* No. 2, 1968, p. 12. The author also points out that "the greater the inflation, the larger, on the average, is the depreciation, even in real terms."

45. This is not the place to undertake an explanation of the technical aspects of credit and money expansion. The interested reader should consult a standard textbook on money and credit. An elementary in-

troduction to this subject may be found in Peter L. Bernstein, *Primer on Money, Banking, and Gold,* New York, 1965.

46. Joint Economic Committee of the Congress of the United States, *Hearings on The Monetary System: Functioning and Possible Reform,* Washington, D.C., 1963, Part 3, p. 551.

47. Joint Economic Committee of the Congress of the United States, *Hearings on the United States Balance of Payments,* Washington, D.C., 1963, Part I, pp. 83-84. The reference that "somebody had to be the world's banker" has a familiar ring. Yet the way Secretary Dillon phrases his comments is an interesting euphemism. Apparently he cannot think of a capitalist world without some form of imperialist domination or of an economic order without capitalism.

48. Robert V. Roosa, *Monetary Reform for the World Economy,* New York, 1965, p. 9.

49. Same as footnote 47, p. 135.

50. *Ibid.,* p. 147.

51. From a report published under the auspices of the Council of Foreign Relations, Henry G. Aubrey, *op. cit.,* p. 15.

52. Robert V. Roosa, *op. cit.,* pp. 23-24.

53. Eugene A. Birnbaum, *Gold and the International Monetary System: An Orderly Reform,* Princeton Essays in International Finance No. 66, Princeton, April 1968, p. 2. Mr. Birnbaum does make an exception to this generalization—the Bretton Woods conference. However, in the light of subsequent history, one can question whether the facade of internationalist spirit at this conference did not cover up a real power struggle.

For an analysis of some of the underlying issues in the struggles over the international monetary system, see "Gold, Dollars, and Empire" in *Monthly Review,* February 1968, and the following articles in the December 1966 issue of *Monthly Review:* "Weak Reeds and Class Enemies," David Michaels, "The Growing Financial Crisis in the Capitalist World," and Jacob Morris, "The Balance of Payments Crises."

The analysis of this question made by Paul M. Sweezy and Leo Huberman ("Weak Reeds and Class Enemies" mentioned above) stimulated a critical reply by Professor Charles P. Kindleberger, of M.I.T.; and a special Princeton Essay on International Finance (No. 61, August 1967, *The Politics of International Money and World Language*) was devoted to this reply. His argument is concerned with demonstrating that the international status of the dollar ("The dollar is the world unit of account—the standard in which foreign exchange reserves, agricultural prices in the Common Market, contributions to the United Nations budget, and a host of other international monetary units are measured." p. 2) is needed for efficiency. "My reason for wanting to keep the dollar-exchange standard is efficiency." (p. 4) Efficiency for what? This the good professor sees purely in terms of the efficiency of capital transfer and of carrying on existing trade relations. To be sure, the dollar-exchange system is a truly efficient device—especially for mobilizing the resources of the world capital markets to finance the war of devastation against the people of Vietnam.

4

AID AND TRADE

Military Expenditures and the Pax Americana

The highly complex interrelationship between the international monetary system and U.S. financial operations comprises, as we have seen, a series of arrangements which have produced the seeming miracle that the United States has grown richer and more powerful in the face of, and indeed because of, a long-term deficit in its balance of payments. This ironic paradox is possible because the balance-of-payments deficit is used to finance three types of overseas activity which are crucially important to the U.S. world position: private investment, military expenditures, and the government foreign aid program.

These three activities have one common feature: they serve to sustain and enhance *control*. Private investment is geared to *control*: control of raw materials sources and control of markets—both activities inherent to monopoly business in the normal pursuit of larger profits and for the protection of monopoly positions. The military expenditures are also needed for control: to carry on the role of leader and administrator of the imperialist system. Appendix A presents the structure of treaties and other commitments made by the United States in building the *Pax Americana*. (See pp. 203-206.) At this point, we will merely present the case as seen by the U.S. Department of Defense:

We have political and security interests, allies, and military forces spread widely over the non-Communist world. The shift of American interests and commitments from the periphery to the center of the world scene has carried with it a concomitant in-

115

crease in the size and overseas deployment of the Armed Forces necessary to provide for the common defense and support the foreign policy of the United States. . . . In the days when our military needs could be met with a stout defense on the seas and a citizen's army, we lived in a world system compatible with our primary national interests. It was based on the nation-state and presided over by British power. The 20th century has seen the old order disintegrate under the impact of two World Wars, the rise of communism supported by a significant power base in both Europe and Asia, the end of the colonial era leading to the creation of a multitude of weak but strident and nationalistic new nations, and rapid technological change—particularly the development of nuclear weapons. During the same period, the United States and the Soviet Union began to emerge as the two leading powers. One major long-term implication of these events was that U.S. national interest would require us to accept and discharge the broad responsibilities of a world power. A second implication was that *the most pressing of our international interests has become the re-creation of a relative stable world environment —a new equilibrium to replace the one destroyed by the events of the four decades following World War I.*[1] (Emphasis added.)

Robert S. McNamara, while Secretary of Defense, pinpointed the connection between this global activity and the foreign aid program. In an address before the American Society of Newspaper Editors in 1966, he explained why the United States should have an economic aid program in these terms:

Roughly 100 countries today are caught up in the difficult transition to modern societies. There is no uniform rate of progress among them, and they range from primitive mosaic societies fractured by tribalism and held feebly together by the slenderest of political sinews—to relatively sophisticated countries, well on the road to agricultural sufficiency and industrial competence. This sweeping surge of development, particularly across the whole southern half of the globe, has no parallel in history.

It has turned traditionally listless areas of the world into seething cauldrons of change.

On the whole it has not been a very peaceful process. . . . Given the certain connection between economic stagnation and the incidence of violence, the years that lie ahead for the nations in the southern half of the globe are pregnant with violence.

This would be true even if no threat of Communist subversion existed—as it clearly does. . . .

Whether Communists are involved or not, violence anywhere

in a taut world transmits sharp signals through the complex ganglia of international relations; and the security of the United States is related to the security and stability of nations half a globe away.[2]

Foreign Aid: Instrument of Control

Like the other two major balance-of-payments-deficit items, economic and military assistance is designed to serve the aims of control. As stated by President John F. Kennedy: "Foreign aid is a method by which the United States maintains a position of influence and control around the world, and sustains a good many countries which would definitely collapse, or pass into the Communist bloc."[3]

The foreign aid program consists of a wide assortment of loans and gifts, including, in the words of a Presidential Commission, "gifts to prove our esteem for foreign heads of state, hastily devised projects to prevent Soviet aid, gambles to maintain existing governments in power."[4]

These diverse activities can be classified according to their purpose or result as follows:

(1) To implement the world-wide military and political policies of the United States.

(2) To enforce the open-door policy: for freedom of access to raw materials, trade, and investment opportunities for U.S. business.

(3) To ensure that such economic development as does take place in the underdeveloped countries is firmly rooted in capitalist ways and practices.

(4) To obtain immediate economic gains for U.S. businessmen seeking trade and investment opportunities.

(5) To make the receivers of aid increasingly dependent on the U.S. and other capital markets. (The debts created by the loans extended perpetuate the bondage of aid-receivers to the capital markets of the metropolitan centers.)

Implementing U.S. Military and Political Policies

A former member of the Program Coordination Staff of

the Agency for International Development (AID) and currently with the Center for International Affairs at Harvard University, Joan Nelson, summarizes the military and political
objectives of foreign aid as "continued access to military bases
and other strategic facilities located in specific developing countries; maintaining ties with formal allies and strengthening their
defense capacity; delaying recognition of Communist China,
and its admission to the United Nations; discouraging trade,
particularly in strategic goods, with Communist China, Cuba,
and North Vietnam; more generally, encouraging independence
or a pro-Western alignment in the foreign policy positions of
developing countries."[5]

In short, the United States pays good money for its
alliances. There is undoubtedly a close connection (though not
necessarily the only factor) between, on the one hand, the vast
Marshall Plan grants and post-Marshall Plan military aid to
West European allies and, on the other hand, the establishment
and operation of NATO. The connection between aid and military alliances is even more obvious in the case of such countries
as Pakistan and Turkey:

> From a political viewpoint, U.S. military aid has strengthened
> Pakistan's armed services, the greatest stabilizing force in the coun-
> try, and has encouraged Pakistan to participate in collective de-
> fense agreements.[6]

> Turkey, with its population of more than 30 million, for ex-
> ample, has been regarded by U.S. aid givers primarily as a military
> mainstay. Its military prowess has been manifested many times.
> Its geographical position, its willingness to take part in such de-
> fensive pacts as NATO and the Baghdad Pact (CENTO), and
> even its unusual mineral resources all have served to qualify Turkey
> highly for whatever foreign assistance might be offered.[7]

If one pays for alliances one surely must pay for bases.
This is quite clearly so for Spain:

> The use of Spanish bases between 1953 and 1963 was ap-
> proved in an agreement that coincided with Export-Import Bank
> loans amounting to $500 million during the ten-year period. When
> a new five-year agreement was arranged in September 1963,
> further bank loans of $100 million were offered over the next
> few years. . . . Over the period 1949-1962, United States aid to

Spain of all types totalled $1.695 billion, nearly three-quarters of which were in the form of grants, both military and economic.[8]

The sellers of bases know a good thing when they see it. The *New York Times* reported in a dispatch earlier this year, "The Spanish Government is asking the United States for a defense guarantee, an increase in military aid, and a reduction of United States legal jurisdiction over American servicemen as the price for renewing the agreement governing American military bases in Spain."[9] Of course, the financial adjustment sought may reflect more than greed: it may be that the Spanish government is merely seeking a cost-of-living adjustment. According to *The Economist* (London):

"This is an age of inflation," a Spanish official said recently. "Prices are constantly rising—especially of bases." Convinced that French and Arab hostility has increased Spain's value to the Americans, the Spanish authorities hope to squeeze a higher economic and political rent out of Washington for American bases in Spain.[10]

The governments which supply soldiers to fight for the United States in Vietnam also command a price. When President Ferdinand Marcos of the Philippines took office in January 1966, he was faced with a bankrupt treasury. As Marcos reported in his inaugural address, at which Vice President Hubert Humphrey was a guest, "The Government treasury is empty. Only by severe self-denial will there be any hope for recovery within the next year."[11] Yet, despite this virtual bankruptcy (or, as cynics might suspect, because of it), Marcos announced, during Humphrey's repeat visit to Manila, his intention to resurrect the previous administration's Vietnam Aid Bill—a measure providing for Philippine troops to be used in Vietnam.[12] The bill was passed after much debate. Finally, in early September, the first 800 army engineers and security troops left Manila for Saigon. Three days later President Marcos arrived in Washington. According to *The New York Times*, Washington felt "under some obligation to provide Mr. Marcos with an economic counterweight to the political capital he was obliged to sacrifice to get his Congress to authorize the troops."[13] Three days after Marcos's arrival in Washington, it was announced that the United States would "make a heavy increase in its economic assistance to the Philippines."[14]

South Korea, too, understands the financial advantages of alliance with the United States, and explores the possibilities. Heading its report "Fighting Tiger for Rent," *The Economist* informs us:

> South Korea, which Vice President Humphrey will be visiting next Wednesday on his way home, is putting a price on the military help it is giving to the Americans in Vietnam. . . . [Korea] has asked the United States for certain quid pro quos for the troops it has sent. These include the "highest priority" for Korea as a supplier of the war materials the United States is buying for use in Vietnam . . . an increase in the allowance paid to Korean troops in Vietnam; and a rise in American military and economic aid. . . .[15]

It is especially instructive to observe the frank declarations by some administrative officials on the purposes of military aid to Latin America as contrasted, for example, with the traditional rationale for such aid to the Near and Middle East. On the latter, Secretary of Defense McNamara told a House Committee in 1967:

> The Near and Middle East remains of strategic significance to the United States because the area is a political, military, and economic crossroads, and because the flow of Middle East oil is vital to the West. We, accordingly, have a large stake in the area's stability and steady development. We also have a strong interest in maintaining our alliance relationships with Greece, Turkey, and Iran, for these three countries stand between the Soviet Union and the warm water ports and oil resources of the Middle East.[16]

In explaining the reasons for military assistance to Latin America, the Secretary of Defense was considerably more specific:

> Social tensions, unequal distribution of land and wealth, unstable economies, and the lack of broadly based political structures create a prospect of continuing instability in many parts of Latin America. The answer to these and other associated problems, if one is to be found, lies in the Alliance for Progress, to which we and our Latin American friends are devoting large resources. *But the goals of the Alliance can be achieved only within a framework of law and order.*

Our military assistance programs for Latin America thus continue to be directed to the support of internal security and civic action measures.[17] (Emphasis added.)

The Secretary of Defense continued his testimony by describing the sources of the threat to law and order: the Tricontinental Congress and the efforts of Latin American Communist parties to create broad popular "anti-imperialist fronts" while continuing to "penetrate student and other intellectual groups, to control organized labor, and to organize the peasants." Hence:

The need to counter these threats by appropriate means is the basis upon which the fiscal year 1968 military assistance programs for Latin American countries are predicated. More specifically, the primary objective in Latin America is to aid, where necessary, in the *continued development of indigenous military and paramilitary forces capable of providing, in conjunction with police and other security forces, the needed domestic security.*[18] (Emphasis added.)

This is not yet the whole story. One of the activities of the U.S. military assistance program is the training of foreign military personnel. As to Latin America, Secretary McNamara informed Congress:

Probably the greatest return on our military assistance investment comes from the training of selected officers and key specialists at our military schools and training centers in the United States and overseas. These students are hand-picked by their countries to become instructors when they return home. They are the coming leaders, the men who will have the know-how and impart it to their forces. I need not dwell upon the value of having in positions of leadership men who have first-hand knowledge of how Americans do things and how they think. It is beyond price to us to make such friends of such men.[19]

The resulting close and valuable friendships undoubtedly go deeper than merely sentimental values of old school ties—as can be seen from the following statement made by the Chairman of the House Foreign Affairs Committee:

Every critic of foreign aid is confronted with the fact that the Armed Forces of Brazil threw out the Goulart government and that U.S. military aid was a major factor in giving these forces an indoctrination in the principles of democracy and a pro-U.S.

orientation. Many of these officers were trained in the United States under the AID program. They knew that democracy was better than communism.[20]

The symbiosis of U.S. and Latin American generals is evident in the Congressional testimony of General Robert W. Porter, Jr., U.S. Army Commander in Chief, U.S. Southern Command (the "Southern" refers to all territory south of the United States):

The inability of governments to attain a sufficient rate of economic development to meet social pressures, together with high population growth and the continuing migration to the cities, will continue to generate more serious problems. The urban areas will become even more the centers of power, and their masses will become more susceptible to demagogic agitation and Communist exploitation. The Communist movement can be expected to become more aggressive, concentrating more attention on labor, students, and the urban slums. When added to the already-serious situation, this increasing urban threat will create a serious internal security problem for the governments of Latin America.

The military has frequently proven to be the most cohesive force available to assure public order and support of resolute governments attempting to maintain internal security. Latin American armed forces, acting in conjunction with the police and other security forces, have helped to control disorders and riots, contained or eliminated terrorists and guerrillas, and discouraged those elements which are tempted to resort to violence to overthrow the government.[21]

Perhaps this is the reason that the Legislative Reference Service of the Library of Congress, in a report prepared for the Senate Foreign Relations Committee, concludes: "There can be little question but that numerous countries are receiving military aid, not because of any direct contribution they might make to the military defense of the United States, or because of their strategic geography, but because there is a political reason for cultivating the generals and admirals in power."[22]

Economic Aid for the Open Door Policy

The reason so much attention has been given to the military aspects of foreign aid is that, despite the official figures which show that most of the aid is economic rather than military, the truth is that the bulk of the aid is ultimately either military or for immediate political aims. The Library of Congress report, referred to above, estimates that only "between one quarter and one third of the $115 billion that has been spent for foreign aid since the close of World War II—including food for peace, Export-Import Bank loans, and other categories— has been devoted to economic development, as such."[23]

Roads (e.g., the road from Saraburi to Ban Phai in Thailand), airports, and communications centers are considered part of economic development assistance, but are frequently geared primarily to military needs. In addition, "more than half a dozen developing countries received substantial economic assistance annually as more or less explicit rental for U.S. military bases or communications centers on their soil."[24]

Summary data on both economic and military aid are shown in Tables XXIII and XXIV. The first of these presents information for the entire period from July 1, 1945 to June 30, 1967. The foreign aid expenditures have been distributed here into three groups. Thirty-nine percent of the aid given for the period as a whole went to developed nations—the senior partners in the imperialist network. This was of course heavily influenced by the Marshall Plan—the major thrust to preserve the capitalist system in a postwar crisis-ridden world. The next largest amount went to a group of countries which we designate as "client" states. These are what government officials call the "forward defense nations" (the countries on the perimeter of the Soviet Union and China) and some of the countries receiving aid in payment for military bases. Finally, some 30 percent of all aid—military and economic—went to the remaining underdeveloped countries where 70 percent of the non-communist world population is located.

The distribution of aid is still strangely askew, even if we consider only the more recent period, long after Marshall Plan aid has stopped. Thus, as shown in Table XXIV, the developed nations received 13 percent of U.S. aid in the ten years from 1957 to 1967. This was primarily military assistance and Export-Import Bank loans. The "client" countries, with 13 percent of the population, received 37 percent of the funds allocated. Only half of the aid during this period went to the other

TABLE XXIII
U.S. ECONOMIC AND MILITARY AID[a]
JULY 1, 1945 TO JUNE 30, 1967

To	*AID* Billion $	Percent of Total	1965 Population In Millions	Percent of Total
Developed Countries[b]	45.7	39	383	19
"Client" Countries[c]	36.9	31	225	11
All other under-developed countries	34.6	30	1,388	70
Total	117.2	100	1,996	100

(a) Total aid, except for grants from excess military stocks, to all non-Communist nations. Does not include some $7 billion of non-regional aid expenditures, such as administrative expenses, aid to "escapees and refugees," contributions to the World Bank, Asian Development Bank, etc.
(b) Western Europe (except Spain and Portugal), Japan, Australia, New Zealand, and Republic of South Africa.
(c) Countries which the United States regards as having special military importance to its policy of containment, including those which have contributed land for bases on their territory: Greece, Iran, Turkey, Vietnam, Formosa, Korea, Philippines, Thailand, Spain, Portugal, Laos. (Included here are regional expenditures for the Southeast Asia region. Excluded are expenditures for the war in Vietnam which are covered from the Department of Defense budget.)
Source: Calculated from data in Statistics and Reports Division, Agency for International Development, *U.S. Overseas Loans and Grants, Obligations and Loan Authorizations*, July 1, 1945—July 30, 1967, Washington, D.C., March 29, 1968.

TABLE XXIV
U.S. ECONOMIC AND MILITARY AID[a]
JULY 1, 1957 TO JUNE 30, 1967

To	Billion $	Percent of Total
Developed Countries[b]	7.5	13
"Client" Countries[c]	20.7	37
All other underdeveloped countries	27.8	50
Total	56.0	100

Footnotes and Source: Same as Table XX.

underdeveloped nations, and even here a substantial amount went for various forms of military assistance—including such activities as the training of Latin American and other military personnel noted above.

It is instructive to evaluate the uses to which even "pure" economic assistance is put. The main drift was neatly summarized in a House Committee on Foreign Affairs report which, after listing a number of reasons for the economic assistance program, concluded: "The most important reason is that nations are determined to develop. Only by participation in that process will we have an opportunity to direct their development along lines that will best serve our interests."[25]

As a latecomer on the colony-grabbing scene (having had its hands full getting hold of and developing the territory on the North American continent), the United States has followed a policy with respect to the rest of the world known as "The Open Door." This took two forms: (a) opening the door in as yet non-colonized territories for trade and investment, and (b) pressuring the colonial empires for equal rights to trade and invest for U.S. business. Thus one of the earliest pressures applied by the New Deal government in the midst of Britain's war against Germany was to call for the elimination of preferences given to Great Britain's businessmen in the British Empire—to open the door for equal treatment for U.S. business. The U.S. loan advanced to rescue Britain's economy at the end of the Second World War was predicated on the removal in Britain's empire of discriminatory practices against outsiders.[26]

It is therefore not surprising to find that one of the major uses of the foreign aid program is to serve the same end. Confronted with shortages of foreign currency and wishing to develop their own industrial economies, underdeveloped countries will frequently set up defense barriers against indiscriminate inflow of imports. This is not an extraordinary procedure. The United States, from the days of Alexander Hamilton, has used trade barriers to protect and stimulate domestic development and to this day is a prominent practitioner of import restrictions through the use of tariffs and quotas. When it comes to the underdeveloped countries, however, the United States firmly adheres to the open door policy. One of the major areas of advice and guidance by Agency for International Development (AID) administrators is to prod aid-recipients to open up the market for imports. Discussing the subtleties of the pressure exerted by AID on aid recipients, *The Economist* (London) observes: "No problems need arise where India's own wishes coincide with what aid-givers want it to do—as, for example . . . accepting a scheme of liberal imports of raw materials and components as a *quid pro quo* for larger maintenance aid."[27]

A major beneficiary of this prodding for the liberalization of imports has been Pakistan. It is true that as a result of this prodding, supported by the injection of U.S. aid, the utilization of Pakistan's productive capacity has improved. A more liberal import policy also opened up some nice opportunities for a wide range of business for foreigners. According to a 1967 article in *International Affairs* (published by Great Britain's Royal Institute of International Affairs) one can now buy in Karachi the following drinks made with imported concentrates: Bubble Up, Canada Dry, Citra, Coca Cola, Double Kola, Kola Kola, Fanta, Hoffman's Mission, Pepsi Cola, Perri Cola, and Seven Up. "At the same time, there are only three sources of bottled milk supply in the city, of which two are commercial and one is publicly owned but of restricted application."[28]

The second aspect of the open door policy—freedom of entry for private investment—undoubtedly ranks higher on the order of priorities of U.S. foreign policy. President Eisenhower thought this issue important enough to include it in his 1953 State of the Union message: "A serious and explicit purpose of our foreign policy [is] the encouragement of a hospitable climate for investment in foreign nations."[29]

The application of this policy is eminently fair, conforming closely to the principle enunciated by Anatole France: "The law in its majestic equality forbids the rich as well as the poor to sleep under bridges, to beg in the streets and to steal bread." This same equality is shown in treaties with underdeveloped countries on rights of investment. Thus, the United States Trade Treaty with the Philippines (the Laurel-Langley Agreement) provides:

The Republic of the Philippines and the United States of America each agrees not to discriminate in any manner, with respect to their engaging in business activities, against the citizens or any form of business enterprise owned or controlled by citizens of the other. . . .

The disposition, exploitation, development, and utilization of all agricultural, timber, and mineral lands of the public domain, waters, minerals, coal, petroleum and other mineral oils, all forces and sources of potential energy, and other natural resources of either Party, and the operation of public utilities, shall, if open to any person, be open to citizens of the other Party. . . .[30]

The legal framework for the open door with respect to capital investment has been incorporated during the post-war era in multilateral agreements, such as the one signed by 20 American nations at Bogota in 1948, and in modernized bilateral Treaties of Friendship, Commerce, and Navigation. The latter treaties contain an investment clause covering the right of United States capital to enter freely into business, non-discrimination against U.S. investors, non-interference with ownership and management operations of U.S. investors, and similar protective provisions. At least eight such full-fledged open-door treaties have been signed: with Ethiopia, Greece, Iran, Israel, Korea, Muscat and Oman, Nicaragua, and Pakistan.

Treaties of this type are often embarrassing to ruling political parties in underdeveloped countries. While the United States has agreed to introduce some flexibility in treaties with underdeveloped countries to accommodate to the political needs of ruling groups in these countries, it insists on having such treaties and uses economic aid as a weapon in obtaining additional treaties to protect U.S. investments. This is done in connection with the Investment Guaranty Program, which is administered by AID. The Investment Guaranty Program provides insurance for U.S. citizens and corporations investing abroad against losses due to nationalization and inability to convert income to U.S. dollars. This insurance program is not available for any country which does not sign an Investment Guaranty Treaty with the United States. As a final pressure to get such treaties in force, the Foreign Assistance Act of 1963 provided that: "No assistance shall be provided under this Act after December 31, 1965 to the government of any less-developed country which has failed to enter into an agreement with the President to institute the investment guaranty program . . . providing against the specific risks of inconvertibility . . . and expropriation or confiscation. . . ."[31]

By now, investment guaranty treaties have been signed with more than 70 underdeveloped countries receiving U.S. aid.

Treaties, apparently, are not sufficient by themselves. An effective open door has to be supervised on a day-to-day basis. Secretary of State Dean Rusk explained this as follows to a Congressional Committee:

We don't challenge in the strictest constitutional sense the right of a sovereign government to dispose of properties and people within its sovereign territory. . . . We do think as a matter of policy it would be wise and prudent on their side to create conditions which will be attractive to the international investor, the private investor. So our influence is used wherever it can be and persistently, through our Embassies on a day-to-day basis, in our aid discussion and in direct aid negotiation, to underline the importance of private investment.[32]

The influence Secretary Rusk refers to is not confined to theoretical discussions on the theory of development. For example, aid was withheld or withdrawn in the case of (a) Ceylon when it nationalized 63 gasoline stations owned by Esso Standard Eastern and Caltex Ceylon, and (b) Peru when a new administration tried to withdraw tax concessions originally granted to the International Petroleum Corporation, a subsidiary of Standard Oil of New Jersey.[33]

Nor did the United States government appreciate the restrictions India wanted to apply to a fertilizer plant investment contemplated by Standard Oil of Indiana. In this case, the weapon was manipulation of the distribution of "food for peace" to hungry India. According to Forbes Magazine:

For a long time India insisted that it handle all the distribution of fertilizer produced in that country by U.S. companies and that it also set the price. Standard of Indiana understandably refused to accept these conditions. AID put food shipments to India on a month-to-month basis until the Indian government let Standard of Indiana market its fertilizer at its own prices.[34]

None of this pressure and inducement would be complete unless it also paved the way for obtaining the raw materials required for monopoly business operations. Thus, the Assistant Secretary of State for African Affairs explains the reasons for granting aid to African nations:

Their good will toward our country is great and we warmly reciprocate this feeling. *Their respect for our interests is illustrated by their special facilities and rights made available to us, by our development of Africa's important mineral and other resources,* to mutual benefit and by political cooperation. American civil and military aircraft use African airspace; U.S. naval ships call at African ports; and the United States maintains space-tracking and communications facilities on African soil. U.S. investment in Africa has doubled in the last decade and has been involved in Africa's major output of such strategic materials as copper, bauxite, iron ore, uranium, petroleum, manganese, and scarce minerals.[85] (Emphasis added.)

Foreign Aid and United States Business

While foreign aid covers an assortment of governmental activities and is used for a complex of economic, military, and political controls in the underdeveloped world, the business community derives direct benefits of an immediate as well as of a long-term nature from this activity. Let us take, for example, the iron and steel industry. One is inclined to think of this industry as part of the backbone of Big Business, hardly a business that needs government subsidies. Take note, then, of this statement by Charles B. Baker, administrative vice president of the United States Steel Corporation:

. . . it is largely due to the operation of our foreign aid program that *the steel industry has managed to escape the full effects of the forces at work in the world market place.* We estimate that AID procurement in the United States of steel mill products currently accounts for some 30 percent of the value of our steel exports, and for an even higher percent of the tonnage shipped— perhaps as much as 40 percent.[86] (Emphasis added.)

The estimates made by the AID statisticians, on which Table XXV is based, do not reach as high a percentage as does Mr. Baker, but high enough. Of the selected commodities on the list, only fertilizer and railroad transportation equipment exports show a higher benefit from government-subsidized exports than does the iron and steel products group. The data for

TABLE XXV
U.S. EXPORTS FINANCED BY AID
1965

Commodity Group	U.S. Exports Total	U.S. Exports Financed by AID	Percent of Exports Financed
		(Million $)	by AID
Machinery and equipment	6,302	333	5.3
Iron and steel mill products	689	168	24.4
Chemicals	2,037	112	5.5
Motor vehicles, engines and parts	1,972	91	4.6
Fertilizer	230	70	30.4
Nonferrous metals	625	72	11.5
Rubber and products	344	33	9.6
Petroleum and products, excluding gas	483	36	7.5
Basic textiles	571	31	5.4
Railroad transportation equipment	146	43	29.5

Source: Charles D. Hyson and Alan M. Strout, "Impact of Foreign Aid on U.S. Exports," *Harvard Business Review*, January-February 1968, p. 71.

the other groups are also respectable and important. The importance of even the lower percentage, say 5 or 6 percent, should not be underestimated. A business firm fights hard for that extra 5 percent of its business, and it usually means much more than 5 percent of the profits counted at the end of the year.

As is well known, the government-supported export of agricultural products is also substantial. From Table XXVI, we can see that 30 percent of all agricultural exports are created by the foreign aid program. In some products—wheat, rice, and dairy products—the ratio is substantially higher. But even for such an important crop as tobacco, foreign aid accounts for 14 percent of the amount exported. (Government support of agricultural exports goes much further. There are, for example, the items mentioned in the footnote to Table XXVI. Of further importance is the fact that if the foreign-aid-sponsored exports were sold in normal channels of trade, the world market prices would drop sharply and thus severely cut the income on the 70 percent of the exports sold "commercially.")

This does not exhaust the extent of business subsidy given by the aid program. Aid-sponsored commodities are required in most instances to be shipped in U.S. flag vessels. The advantage to U.S. shipping can be quite substantial. Thus, on 18 large locomotives shipped under the aid program, the Pakistan government paid 113 percent more in freight charges to a U.S.

TABLE XXVI
U.S. AGRICULTURAL EXPORTS
1955 TO 1966

		Amount (billion $) Government Financed[a]	Commercial[b]		Percent Distribution Government Financed[a]	Commercial[b]
	Total			Total		
All Agricultural Exports	57.6	17.2	40.4	100	30	70
Selected Products						
Wheat and Wheat Flour	12.2	8.3	3.9	100	68	32
Rice, Milled	1.7	.7	1.0	100	41	59
Cotton	8.0	2.6	5.4	100	32	68
Dairy Products	2.3	1.3	1.0	100	57	43
Tobacco, unmanufactured	4.4	.6	3.8	100	14	86

(a) Included here are only the government financed exports under the two specific programs which are connected with economic and military assistance: Public Law 480 shipments and Mutual Security (AID) shipments.

(b) Commercial sales include in addition to unassisted commercial transactions, shipments of some commodities with governmental assistance in the form of (1) extension of credit and credit guaranties, (2) sales of government-owned commodities at less than domestic market prices and (3) payments to exporters to compensate them for the difference between domestic and world prices. An average of 30 percent of dollar exports of U.S. farm products received the latter form of assistance.

Source: Economic Research Service, U.S. Department of Agriculture, *12 Years of Achievement under Public Law 480*, Washington, D.C., November 1967.

flag ship than it would have had to pay if it had been free to accept the lowest bid received. On the movement of 20 small locomotives, the extra payment to a U.S. shipping line amounted to 62 percent.[37] The general effect of these indirect subsidies is described in a *Harvard Business Review* article:

> Although AID is not involved in direct subsidization of exports, U.S. procurement policies do in effect provide indirect subsidies to U.S. exporters. This is because some of our tied exports would simply not occur if it were not for foreign assistance financing. This is most easily seen in the case of a number of U.S. commodities that are priced above world levels but which are nevertheless exported because AID funds are restricted for purposes of their purchase. The cost of some commodities we finance may run considerably above world market prices.[38]

This type of preferential trade regulations and subsidies is characteristic also of aid given by other advanced countries. Professor Edward S. Mason, of Harvard, in his book *Foreign Aid and Foreign Policy,* discusses these various forms of subsidy and notes that it would be impossible to find a quantitative formula that takes them all into account. "But," says he, "I might hazard the guess that if it could be done, it would boil the nearly $9 billion in total flow of funds from the developed to the underdeveloped world to a figure in the range of $2 billion to $3 billion."[39] (Professor Mason included in his estimate not only the higher prices of tied aid, shipping charges, artificial import and export prices in the franc zone, but also the effect which would be produced by all U.S. non-commercial exports of agricultural products if they were offered for commercial sale.)

We have not come to the end of our list of business stimuli arising from aid activities. There is also the business created by the long-lasting influence of military assistance. One necessary result of the military assistance program and the military coordination on the several regional military treaties is the standardization of armaments used by the recipient countries. This is not only a policy question, but a practical matter. Once an army is supplied with a given assortment of equipment, the ammunition and the replacement and expansion requirements will be most efficiently met from the same source. The result is continuing good business for U.S. armaments manufacturers. This profitable business derives not only from the sale of exports but also in the form of royalties from licenses:

The expansion and standardization of NATO armaments has opened new areas for licensing abroad. U.S. companies which are producing particular types of material for use by the U.S. armed forces have been requested to supply technical information and extend patent rights so that similar equipment may be produced in Europe. The U.S. government freely licenses its proprietary rights in any developments made under government contract, but the commercial rights must be extended from the U.S. company to the foreign company or government under contract. The manufacture of tanks, jets, engines, firearms, and other equipment has increased the demand for licenses; *the contacts have also been the basis for wider agreements on non-military items.*[40] (Emphasis added.)

This intertwining of government and business activity extends beyond military hardware. Eugene R. Black, former president of the World Bank, claims that "replacements and additions for India's railroads are being purchased mainly from the United States, because AID-financed locomotives were provided back in the 1950's."[41] President Kennedy also recognized the longer-term implications of U.S. aid:

The President cited the cases of Taiwan, Colombia, Israel, Iran, and Pakistan as examples of nations whose import patterns had been drastically affected by foreign aid. "These used to be the exclusive market of European countries," Mr. Kennedy said. "Too little attention has been paid to the part which an early exposure to American goods, skills, and American ways of doing things can play in forming the tastes and desires of newly emerging countries—or to the fact that, even when our aid ends, the desire and need for our products continue, and trade relations last far beyond the termination of our assistance.[42]

An idea of the extent to which foreign aid has enabled U.S. business to penetrate the former preserves of the European powers can be gained from Table XXVII. Thus, before the war, the U.S. accounted for some 6 percent of the imports into India and Pakistan. (Pakistan and India were one country then; therefore the figure for India in 1938 applies to both countries.) Now, between 30 and 40 percent of the imports to these countries comes from the United States. Turkey, to take another case, bought about 11 percent of its foreign goods from the United States before the war; now the U.S. share is almost 27 percent. Nigeria was pretty much outside the U.S. area of interest before the war. Today, the United States gets some 16 percent of Nigeria's business.

TABLE XXVII
U.S. SHARE OF EACH COUNTRY'S IMPORTS

(Percent of total imports)

	1938	1952	1966
India	6.4	34.4	41.7
Pakistan[a]		6.0	32.4
Australia	15.6	14.5	23.3
Greece	7.3	21.8	11.7
Turkey	10.5	8.4	26.8
Iran	8.4	22.4	20.0
Spain	10.5[b]	16.7	17.4
Nigeria	5.8	4.6	15.8

(a) Included with India in 1938.
(b) 1937.
Source: Calculated from data in *International Trade Statistics 1938,* Geneva, League of Nations, 1939; *Directory of International Trade,* Washington, D. C. International Monetary Fund, Vol. IV, 1953 and Vol. V, 1954; *Direction of Trade 1962-1966,* Washington, D. C., International Monetary Fund, 1966.

African markets, in particular, seem to be opening up new opportunities for U.S. business. A 1968 report from AID to a Congressional Committee reads:

While Africa currently represents less than $1 out of every $20 of U.S. foreign trade, this proportion has been growing at over 10 percent annually—double the rate of U.S. trade increases with the rest of the developing world. Of that total, United States exports to less-developed African states (over $750 million in 1967) have more than doubled since 1960 and have grown at a faster rate than have exports to South Africa.

Underlying these statistics is a marked shift from the traditional African dependence on European suppliers. Commercial U.S. exports to African aid recipients have increased by more than 55 percent in recent years.[43]

As for Latin America, one of the achievements of the Alliance for Progress, according to the State Department, is that "the United States has been able to protect its share [of the trade of the industrial countries] and even increase it at the expense of the other industrial countries."[44]

The influence of foreign assistance in expanding normal business channels can also be seen in agriculture, as reported by the Agriculture Department:

One of the major objectives of the P.L. [Public Law] 480 program and an important measure of the success of foreign policy goals is the transition of countries from food aid to commercial trade. Japan, which during 1956 and 1957 received over 30 percent of its imports of U.S. farm products under P.L. 480, increased its U.S. dollar purchases from around $300 million in those years to more than $900 million in 1966, and has been the largest dollar market for the products of American farms for a number of years. During 1955-61, Italy received substantial quantities of agricultural commodities under P.L. 480 and Mutual Security programs. Dollar sales of U.S. farm products to Italy increased from over $36 million in 1955 to nearly $275 million in 1966. Another example of the transition from "AID" to "trade" may be found in Spain, which during 1956-62 received from $61 to $141 million annually in U.S. food aid. Since 1956, Spain's dollar purchases increased from $10 million to nearly $200 million in 1966.[45]

In addition to opening up trade channels and subsidizing business opportunities in export lines, the foreign aid program also gives a boost to U.S. foreign investment. First, there is the general area of support and protection. As Assistant Secretary of Commerce Andrew F. Brimmer pointed out in an address to a meeting of businessmen, "if these aid programs were discontinued, private investments might be a waste, because it would not be safe enough for you to make them."[46]

In particular, there is the pressure on the aid recipients to sign treaties in support of investment guaranty agreements, as mentioned above. This is to create the proper protective legal environment for private investment from the United States. The foreign aid program even pays for travel and other expenses of U.S. business firms who wish to look into business investment opportunities. And, in some cases, a U.S. management consultant firm is given a contract by AID to explore the field. One such contract was given to Arthur D. Little, Inc. to promote investment in Nigeria. Among the results were help and advice to start the following enterprises in Nigeria: a Colgate Palmolive International plant to make detergents and tooth paste, an Aba Textile Mills (Indian Head Mills) plant to establish the first cotton textile print plant in Nigeria, and a Union Carbide plant to make dry-cell batteries.[47]

Foreign Aid: The White Man's Burden

When Lord Balfour was challenged in the House of Commons about Britain's usurping the government of Egypt, he explained that British wisdom was necessary to replace the incompetence of Egyptian rulers:

Western nations as soon as they emerge into history show the beginnings of those capacities for self-government, not always associated, I grant, with all the virtues or all the merits, but still having merits of their own. . . . You may look through the whole history of the Orientals in what is called, broadly speaking, the East, and you never find traces of self-government. All their great centuries—and they have been very great—have been passed under despotisms, under absolute government. . . . Conqueror has succeeded conqueror; one domination has followed another; but never in all the revolutions of fate and fortune have you seen one of these nations of its own motion establish what we, from a Western point of view, call self-government. . . . I suppose a true Eastern sage would say that the working government which we have taken upon ourselves in Egypt and elsewhere is not a task worthy of a philosopher—that it is dirty work, the inferior work, of carrying on the necessary labor. . . . The time may come when they will adopt, not merely our superficial philosophy, but our genuine practice. But after 3,000, 4,000, or 5,000 years of known history have been passed by these nations under a different system, it is not thirty years of British rule which is going to alter the character bred into them by immemorial tradition.

If that be true, is it or is it not a good thing for these great nations—I admit their greatness—that this absolute government should be exercised by us? I think it is a good thing. I think that experience shows that they have got under it a far better government than in the whole history of the world they ever had before, and which not only is a benefit to them, but is undoubtedly a benefit to the whole of the civilized West.[48]

Lord Balfour could probably never have imagined that the British bearer of the white man's burden would become the weak

link in the imperialist chain—forced to devalue its currency time
and again, financially incompetent to maintain key military
bases, and beginning to question its ability to maintain sterling
as a reserve currency. The dirty work of sustaining Western
civilization for the benefit of the underdeveloped world and for
the civilized West now lies heavily on the conscience of the
United States. The absence of political control via colonies calls
for greater ingenuity and sophistication, not to mention pas-
sionate commitment.

The great financial resources of the United States—not
limitless, to be sure, but enhanced by the concentration of world
banking within its borders and by the credit expansion possible with the dollar as an international currency—are of the
greatest utility for these purposes. The simplest element in this
operation is to pay off friendly governments and to assist them
to stay in power. Often, reading the statistics of government aid
agencies is like reading a political barometer. Take the case of
AID expenditures in Brazil, shown in Table XXVIII.

What happened before 1964, when AID expenditures
dropped so sharply? The United States became increasingly
dissatisfied with the economic and political actions of the Goulart

TABLE XXVIII
EXPENDITURES IN BRAZIL BY AGENCY FOR
INTERNATIONAL DEVELOPMENT

Fiscal Year Ending June 30	Expenditures (millions of dollars)
1962	$ 81.8
1963	38.7
1964	15.1
1965	122.1
1966	129.3

Source: Statistics and Reports Division, Agency for International Development, *U. S. Economic Assistance Programs Administered by the
Agency for International Development and Predecessor Agencies,
April 3, 1943—June 30, 1966,* Washington, D. C., March 30,
1967, p. 28.

regime. What happened in Brazil in 1964? The Goulart government was overthrown by military officers friendly to and trained

by the United States, as explained in the statement of the Chairman of the House Foreign Affairs Committee cited above. The data in Table XXVIII are only one aspect of the spurt in financial aid supplied to the new government: other agencies in addition to AID were also active. The United States committed itself in 1964 alone to giving and lending over $500 million to the new regime. In addition, as a former high AID official tells us, "multilateral institutions [e.g., World Bank and IMF] were successfully encouraged to supplement this sum."[49]

This type of control is fairly simple. But life is usually more complicated for the administrators of United States policy. Jacob J. Kaplan, formerly Assistant Coordinator for Foreign Assistance in the Department of State, explains the nature of these complexities with special reference to the case of Chile:

During 1965, the United States wanted the government of Chile to check the rate of inflation, support the establishment of an inter-American military force, oppose the admission of Red China to the United Nations, accelerate the reform of its tax-collection arrangements, and reach a workable agreement with its embattled U.S.-owned copper companies. The list is not exhaustive, but each of these steps was important to one or another basic U.S. interest. Each raised difficulties for the Chilean government.

The Christian Democratic government had taken office in 1964 after a closely contested electoral victory over Communist-supported opposition. Its program had called for agricultural and tax reform; but also for re-examination of traditional Chilean acceptance of U.S. foreign policy leadership. It was representative of reform-minded opposition to the conservative oligarchy that had long controlled the country. Despite heavy concentration of U.S. aid funds in previous years, economic growth had averaged only 3 percent a year and living costs had risen 45 percent in 1963 and 39 percent in 1964. Continued U.S. aid in substantial amounts was essential to the success of the new government's program for modernizing Chile through evolutionary processes.

U.S. officials undoubtedly pressed for all five points without any clear demonstration of its priorities. Chile abstained on the U.N. vote to seat Red China, the first time it had failed to add its vote to that of the United States and most of its Latin American neighbors in support of Taiwan's right to the Chinese seat. On the more critical question of whether the admission of Red China was sufficiently important to require the endorsement of two-thirds of the U.N. General Assembly, Chile joined the United States in registering an affirmative vote.[50]

Interlarded as the foreign aid program is with bureaucratic complications, the patina of a humanitarian rationale, and the idiosyncracies of U.S. political structure (executive-legislative-judicial balance), the variations in foreign aid practices over the years may seem confusing. But throughout all its variations there are two dominant and interrelated ends toward which the control and influence is exercised: (a) to keep the outer rim of the imperialist network as dependencies of the system, and (b) to sustain and stimulate the growth of capitalist forces—economic and political—within these countries.

One example of the way the first aim is pursued can be seen in the incorporation into the basic foreign assistance law of a directive that the underdeveloped countries should be kept dependent on "free world" sources of fuel—often the lifeblood of the underdeveloped countries' economy:

It is of paramount importance that long-range economic plans take cognizance of the need for a dependable supply of fuels, which is necessary to orderly and stable development and growth, and that dependence not be placed upon sources which are inherently hostile to free countries and the ultimate well-being of economically underdeveloped countries and which might exploit such dependence for ultimate political domination. The agencies of government in the U.S. are directed to work with other countries in developing plans for basing development programs on the use of the large and stable supply of relatively low-cost fuels available in the free world.[51]

With respect to the second aim, the following excerpts from AID reports illustrate the kind of pressures which are brought to bear to secure greater freedom for capitalist enterprise:

The Bolivian government also initiated strong measures to reform and reorganize the nationalized tin mines, passed a revised mining code favorable to private investment, issued a decree for the consolidation and control of the budgets and foreign borrowings of the semi-autonomous government corporations, and promulgated a new investment code and a revised, and more equitable, royalties schedule designed to encourage private investment. Each of these self-help measures had been strongly urged by AID, and their adoption is largely attributable to AID assistance.[52]

The Castello Branco administration [of Brazil] has conducted an effectively tough economic program of stabilization, development, and reform. . . . Private enterprise has been encouraged by policies halting the previous trend toward state ownership. New incentives have been created and old obstacles removed in an effort to increase the participation of private enterprise, both foreign and domestic. New foreign investment is being sought for development of minerals and petrochemicals, and an Investment Guaranty agreement has been signed with the United States.[53]

Private enterprise has greater opportunities in India than it did a few years ago. . . . There are still more sectors of the economy in which private enterprise has a hard time, but fertilizer is an example of a field which is now open to the private sector, and was not in the past. This is largely a result of the efforts which we have made, the persuasion that we along with other members at the consortium have exerted on the Indian government. We feel that conditions in India are improving steadily. They still have not gone as far as we would like to see them go.[54]

The mechanics of control over the direction of economic development are too various and involved to be elaborated in the space available here. U.S. officials necessarily participate at practically every level of a recipient's decision-making in the realm of economic affairs; they try to build up alliances with the most reliable pro-U.S. officials (often those educated and trained in the United States, with AID assistance); resident advisers and technicians are supplied. The ultimate, no doubt, is reached when, as in the case of Greece, a contract is made by the Greek government with a U.S. corporation (Litton International Corporation) to take over the economic development programming for the entire island of Crete.

One particular form of control should be specifically mentioned, since it is probably little known and little understood. When aid is in the form of commodities financed by a U.S. loan, the receiving government is frequently required to deposit in a counterpart fund the income it receives from selling these commodities in local markets. About 10 percent of the receipts is turned over to the U.S. government for payment of local expenses of the U.S. embassy, missions from the United States, or perhaps travelling Congressmen. The remaining 90 percent remains in the possession of the local government but can only be used for expenditures agreed to by the United States.

In addition, agricultural products shipped to the under-developed countries (under P.L. 480) are also sold within each country through normal trade channels. The income from these sales, however, belongs to the U.S. government. These U.S.-owned local currencies derive from other foreign aid programs as well, but the largest part arises from the P.L. 480 sales. This money is then used for internal purposes: loans are made to the government and others. These hoards of currency keep on growing, since interest is paid on the loans. In many countries they assume quite large proportions. The manner in which these very substantial funds are handled can seriously affect the freedom of action of the recipient government's economic authorities. The extent of these U.S.-owned and -controlled currencies can be seen from the following examples:

Huge blocked rupee funds, credited to the United States government, have accumulated in India and Pakistan as a result of repayment in local currency of old-style Development Loan Fund "soft" loans and especially sales of surplus food grains provided under P.L. 480 loans. Professor Lewis has estimated that by the end of the Third Plan, United States rupee holdings in India "are likely to have an aggregate value of Rs. 800 to 900 crores," which "might be equivalent to, say, one fifth of the total Indian money supply." This estimate, startling as it is, was too conservative. By January 1964, more than two years before the end of India's Third Five Year Plan, the blocked rupee holdings of the United States government had exceeded 1100 crores of rupees ($2.3 billion).[55]

From the point of view of the [Pakistan] State Bank's monetary policy, it is, of course, very undesirable for a third party [the U.S. government] to own as much as 15 percent of the total money supply and to have unilateral control over almost 8 percent unless there is a clear understanding between the two governments about the handling of these funds. Under present conditions, it is possible that the effectiveness of any action by the State Bank to restrict credit could be impaired through independent transactions made by the U.S. government. Such action need not be premeditated as was suggested by the press.[56]

At the present rate of flow of surplus commodities, together with repayments of previous loans [from the U.S. to the Egyptian government], counterpart funds and outstanding loans to the government will mount in ten years to a magnitude comparable with the present [Egyptian] government budget.[57]

In carrying out its policies, the United States works in co-operation with such international organizations as the International Monetary Fund (IMF)—a major source of short-term loans for deficit countries—and the International Bank for Reconstruction and Development (hereafter referred to as IBRD or World Bank)—an important source for long-term funds. In addition, there is the coordinating group of the leading industrial nations, called the Development Assistance Committee, and made up of the United States, Canada, Japan, and the aid-donor countries of Western Europe. (Among other things, "the DAC . . . establishes working groups for intensive consideration of specific assistance problems, such as how to assess a less-developed country's performance and aid requirements, or how to encourage greater private investment in developing countries."[58])

The cooperation between the U.S. foreign aid program and such international institutions is based on the control that the United States and the other leading industrial nations have in these institutions, and the mutual interest of these leading nations (despite competitive struggles among themselves) in preserving a certain type of relationship with the underdeveloped countries. The impact of these organizations working in harness, often as consortia in aid programs, is to impress the recipient countries that there is no recourse other than to follow the advice and instructions of aid and loan givers. For the United States, working with the other countries often serves as a handy tactic: the imposition of the will of the United States does not appear as ominous when it comes under the auspices of an international organization. Professor Mason, who has had much experience in the foreign aid field, observes that

it is usually much easier to bring about changes in domestic policies through the mediation of an international agency such as the International Bank or Monetary Fund than through bilateral stabilization agreements in Latin America. The consortium meetings presided over by the International Bank have come to be the most important forums for criticism of the development programs and policies of India, Pakistan, and other countries financed in this manner . . . if the United States, or any other aid-dispensing country, is to exert influence on the domestic policies of an aid-receiving country, either directly or via an international agency, its representatives must have a clear idea, based on careful analysis, of what it wants this country to do. Frequently, such ideas have been lacking. Recently AID has given increased attention to this problem and has attempted to formulate for some of the principal aid-receiving countries a so-called Long-Range Assistance Strategy which spells out U.S. economic, political, and security interests in the countries in question, the conditions necessary to their attainment, and the relevant instruments of foreign policy.[59]

In its own right, the World Bank exercises simple and direct controls. It withholds and grants loans, as any good banker would, according to its opinion of the reliability of the borrower. Recall the above reference to AID expenditures before and after Goulart. The World Bank too "refused to make any loans to Brazil for several years prior to 1964 mainly because of the unsound financial policies of the government preceding the Branco administration."[60]

The Bank sets rigid conditions of control over independent nations as terms for its loans, dictating, as in the case of the Yanhee Power Project in Thailand, that the government set up a separate Power Board apart from the normal government authority; that all key positions in the electric power authority, including general manager, be made with prior consultation with the Bank; and that no contracts be let without approval of the consulting engineers who in turn must be approved by the World Bank.[61]

Aside from pressuring the borrowers to improve the private investment climate, the World Bank also serves as an unabashed conduit for the movement of private capital to the most choice investment opportunities revealed in negotiations with loan applicants. Professor Baldwin, who is not reluctant to use the term "blackmail," describes in general terms, some of the past activities of the Bank:

The IBRD, in effect, exists to drum up business for its competition, the private investors. In the face of demands from the underdeveloped countries for the maximum amount of capital on the easiest possible terms in the shortest period of time, the IBRD was replying, in effect, that they really did not need as much capital as they imagined; the capital they did need was private, not public; and the reason they were short of private capital was that their governments were following undesirable policies. The solution, therefore, was for the IBRD to withhold loans in a strategic attempt to encourage (blackmail) the government into changing their policies.[62]

To temper the resentment of underdeveloped nations against the heavy-handed control exercised by the World Bank, various new arrangements have been devised, especially the regional development banks. But they too, covered by a façade of "local" control, are subject to the same rigors of economic necessity in the world of finance. The reasons for this are explained by Professor Mikesell:

There is a feeling in many of the less-developed countries that the major international lending institutions are dominated by the United States and other Western Powers and that therefore they seek to impose the policies of the Western industrial countries upon the developing countries of the world. It was partly for this reason that the Latin American republics worked for many years for the establishment of an inter-American financial institution which would be operated by and for Latin Americans. Although to a considerable degree this argument has been based on the dissatisfaction with the lending standards imposed by the International Bank, there may be important political and psychological advantages in channeling a substantial portion of the public capital available for Latin America through the new Inter-American Development Bank. Nevertheless, *because the Inter-American Development Bank must, as must the World Bank, secure its financing from the international capital markets, it must gain the confidence of the U.S. government and the public by means of sound loan operations.* Therefore, if it's to be successful, its policies are not likely to be greatly different from those of the World Bank.[63] (Emphasis added.)

Control Via the IMF

The ultimate discipline imposed by the rich nations on the poor arises from the stabilization loans made by the International Monetary Fund. Here we are no longer dealing with development projects or long-term plans for possible growth. The country that applies to the IMF for a loan (a short-term loan to stabilize its currency) is more often than not in desperate, or close to desperate, straits. The usual sequence is that the

country's balance-of-payments deficit eats up the reserves of
the state treasury or the central bank; the deficit persists; collection notices from foreign sellers cannot be complied with;
payments of interest and amortization on past loans from foreign bankers and governments cannot be made; dividends on
foreign investments cannot be remitted. As a result, the country
faces bankruptcy. Bankruptcy for a country, it should be noted,
is not merely a matter of losing one's good name; it signals the
breakdown of foreign trade and the inability to import foreign
goods necessary for the economic life of the country.

The country affected will try various emergency measures
to get out of the box it finds itself in: controls over imports,
subsidies for exporters, multiple exchange rates as a device for
subsidy and control, etc. But when these fail, or extra cash is
needed to give them a chance to work, the country turns necessarily to the IMF: private bankers are not very reliable lenders
to a customer who can't meet his bills, especially if the bills are
from a fellow banker. The practice of the IMF is to lend the
country virtually on demand up to 25 percent of the country's
quota in the Fund—this is backed up by the collateral of the
country's own gold subscription to the Fund. Beyond this, the
deficit country has to justify its request for a loan. And the
IMF, like any good banker, uses the period of squeeze to insist
that the borrower take action so that he will be a more responsible borrower. A good, conservative banker conserves; in other
words, he helps to maintain the traditional business relations,
including, of course, the continuing economic and financial dependency of the weaker on the stronger nations.

The classic illustration of the IMF-type of control occurred
when the Castro government turned to the IMF and the World
Bank to build up foreign currency reserves that had been de-
pleted by the Batista regime, and to initiate serious industrialization and agricultural reform. *The New York Times* explained
that Cuba could get economic assistance under certain conditions: "If Dr. Castro is to get large-scale aid for his budgetary
and balance-of-payments problems, he will have to agree to a
stabilization program proposed by the International Monetary
Fund. This would involve credit restraint and a balanced—or
nearly balanced—budget."[64]

However, credit restraint and a balanced budget would produce more, not less, unemployment. Even more than that, such rigid restrictions would in effect be a veto on agrarian reform and on measures to eliminate unemployment.

The Cuban response, of course, was to opt out of the imperialist system, seek allies in the socialist camp, and begin to reconstruct its economy along diversified lines, with maximum utilization of its human and natural resources. (It is wrong to confuse economic independence with autarky. The question is not elimination of trade, but the elimination of the extreme reliance on a limited type of trade that serves only to meet the requirements and conditions of the ruling nations.)

But the country that does not seek a wholly different path must be ready to buckle down to the demands of the lender. The IMF as lender to borrowers in distress sets up tough conditions before handing out money, in the best traditions of international banking. IMF circles are not concerned, at least not officially, whether the persistent deficit of some countries may be the necessary consequence of a persistent surplus in other countries and, if so, whether balance can ever be attained if adjustments are not made in the surplus countries (tariff walls, import quotas, and the like) as well as in the deficit countries. By its structure and administrative procedures, the IMF acts only to enforce the rules of the game that governs the existing power relations among countries—*rules that evolved in the very process by which some nations became the rich nations and other nations became the poor nations.* That is why Thomas Balogh, Fellow of Balliol College, Oxford, and since 1964 Economic Adviser to the British Cabinet, evaluates the mechanics of neo-imperialism (as he calls it) thus:

I believe it can be shown that the automatism [of the market] which evolved represents in itself a severe limitation on the possibility of full development of the weaker partner in the "colonial pact," even if there is no conscious policy which aims at exploitation for the benefit of the metropolitan area. Beyond this, the philosophy of monetary and fiscal soundness itself represents a further handicap to the weaker area. If this analysis is correct, two conclusions follow, both unpalatable to current conventional wisdom. The first is that the present upsurge in the ex-colonial areas provides no guarantee of a stable and steady progress in the future unless special efforts are made to substitute positive stimuli for the negative ending of colonial limitation. The second is that neo-imperialism does not depend on open political domination. The economic relations of the U.S. to South America are not essentially different from those of Britain to her African colonies. *The International Monetary Fund fulfills the role of the colonial administration of enforcing the rules of the game.*[65] (Emphasis added.)

The sound monetary and fiscal policies insisted on by the IMF fall into familiar patterns:[66]

(1) Eliminate controls over imports and exports; free exchange rates; devalue the currency to a more realistic exchange rate relative to the dollar. The result of such changes is to reinforce the existing price and trade relationships and all the resulting facets of economic and financial dependency. This is not necessarily by design, or a nefarious plot by a small group of international bankers. This is a straightforward application of "sound" principles of economics and finance: the blind forces of the market place are to work their wonders. However, the blind forces of the market place, when they are efficient, are efficient in reproducing the existing allocation of resources and, equally, in reproducing the inequities of this allocation of resources: inequities within the country and inequities in the relations of the strong nations to the weak.

(2) Inaugurate strong money and fiscal controls within the country; institute wage and price controls; balance the budget. Again, sound and responsible economics. But what does this mean in underdeveloped capitalist nations? Balanced budgets are achieved by increasing taxes and reducing government expenditures. What taxes and whose taxes will be increased in countries dominated by a small ruling elite? On reducing expenditures, the easiest items to cut are welfare expenditures. (This should not seem strange to U.S. readers who witnessed the impact of the Vietnam War on welfare spending.) One of the biggest gripes of the IMF and U.S. AID officials concerns the government corporations in the underdeveloped countries (such as public transportation and electric power) that operate on a deficit. One of the chief demands made by the IMF in

exchange for assistance in stabilizing currencies is the elimination of such deficits. But usually these deficits are a government subsidy to supply electric power and transportation, for example, at rates which lower-income groups can afford. The elimination of the deficits is accomplished by raising prices to a profitable level. As for wage and price controls, no comment need be made on how these habitually work in capitalist nations.

There is no conflict between the aims of the IMF and of AID activity; in fact they work closely together, as evidenced by a former AID official:

The Greek stabilization program in the mid-1950's, and agreements with Brazil, Colombia, and Chile have all been supported by U.S. aid linked to observance of IMF recommendations. In Chile, for example, program loans in 1963 and 1964 were largely conditioned on Chilean compliance with fiscal, monetary, and foreign exchange rate policies defined in Stand-by Agreements with the IMF. More recently, in 1966-67, AID assistance to Ceylon and Ghana was tied to stabilization measures recommended by the Fund. . . .[67]

When the IMF negotiates loans, the imposed conditions get down to very specific commitments the borrowing countries must make. The exchange of letters between the IMF, the United States, and the borrowing country, which reveal the terms dictated, are confidential and difficult for the public to discover. However, one instance that came to the surface is highly illuminating. In 1959, one of the budget-balancing requirements imposed on the Bolivian government was the elimination of superfluities from the budget:

Both International Monetary Fund stabilization assistance and U.S. government aid were negotiated on condition that the government of Bolivia undertake economic stabilization measures, including specifically the elimination of a $3 million a year subsidy to government commissaries selling consumers' goods to miners.[68]

What this elimination of a subsidy for miners' commissaries must have meant can be inferred from the following story in *The New York Times* by Paul Montgomery, headed "Hunger is Constant Companion of Bolivia Miners":

Down a creaking, narrow-gauge track, two Indian miners strained to move a rusted cart full of tin ore.

The ore would eventually find its way to Huanuni, in the valley, then to the concentrating mill near Oruro 20 miles away, then to smelters in the United States or Britain, and then, perhaps, to tin cans for the convenience of housewives and, finally, to garbage heaps to be buried again in the earth.

The Indians pushing the cart, whose basic wage is $25 a month, had probably never eaten anything that comes in a tin can. Their cheeks bulged with their staple food—coca leaves, from which cocaine is extracted.

Bolivian miners chew the leaf, which costs 5 cents for a double handful, because it dampens hunger and gives them energy for work in the thin air.

Behind the one cart, a tiny girl no more than 6 years old trudged along. Her infant brother peered out from the tattered shawl that held him to his sister's back. The little girl's feet were bound in mud-caked rags. Her legs were blue.

She was looking along the track for pieces of ore shaken loose from the carts. If the ore is of high grade, it can be exchanged for food in illicit stores.[69]

Aid and Indebtedness

The economic dependency of the underdeveloped countries as the suppliers of food and raw materials to the developed countries results in financial dependency as well. And this financial dependency serves to cement the economic dependency. This process usually follows the following lines: Fluctuations in the demand for and hence the price of the primary products exported by the underdeveloped countries creates frequent deficits. The deficits are financed by borrowing from the creditor countries. Servicing the debt—payment of interest and amortization—requires that a portion of future exports be devoted to this purpose instead of buying needed imports. Hence, further borrowing is induced to pay for their regular imports. This cycle of economic-financial dependency becomes even more pronounced, paradoxically, as a country tries to advance via the established capitalist path. For then the country imports capital goods from the same creditor nations and goes even further into debt: the capital goods are bought on credit and have to be paid for in the currency of the supplying country.

Developed countries, especially the weaker ones and those still paying for past wars, also have external debts. But the

difference between the advanced countries and the outer rim
of the imperialist network is strikingly revealed in the comparison
of the changes in the external debt positions of these two groups
of nations, as shown in Table XXIX.

TABLE XXIX
ESTIMATED EXTERNAL MEDIUM- AND LONG-TERM PUBLIC DEBT OUTSTANDING

As of January 1	Developed Countries	Underdeveloped Countries
	(Billions of Dollars)	
1956	$14.2	$ 9.7
1960	15.9	16.4
1964	14.9	30.0
1967	16.6	41.5

Source: International Bank for Reconstruction and Development, *External
Medium- and Long-Term Public Debt Past and Projected
Amounts Outstanding, Transactions and Payments: 1956-1976*,
Washington, D.C., December 4, 1967. These data summarize
the debt statistics for 16 developed and 92 underdeveloped
countries. Note: These are estimates. The report is circulated
to libraries and students in the field, with the proviso that they
are not official World Bank figures.

This more than fourfold increase in the external debt of
the underdeveloped countries during the past decade has also
meant a very rapid growth in the servicing requirements: in
1956, the underdeveloped countries as a whole had to pay out
close to $800 million to service their debts, or less than 3 percent
of their exports; in 1967, they had to pay out some $3.9 billion,
or more than 10 percent of their exports.[70] As will be shown
later, the debt burden for many individual countries was much
heavier than indicated by these overall figures.

In this process of debt expansion and increasing burden
of debt service, the aid activities of the industrial nations play
a special role. First, a substantial portion of the aid given goes
to pay previous debt and not current development expenses.
Thus, in 1966 approximately 44 percent of aid flowing from
the advanced to the underdeveloped countries was needed to
finance past debt.[71] Second, the very process of aid-giving increases the debt burdens of the dependent debtor nations.

Let us look at U.S. aid practices to see how this works. Table XXX presents the distribution of U.S. aid in the form of loans and grants for the period from fiscal year 1945 to fiscal year 1967. What we find is that 73 percent of the aid that was given over these years to the advanced industrial partners of the United States was in the form of grants. An even higher percent (87 percent) of the contributions to the "client" states were grants. But when we come to the bulk of the underdeveloped world, only 42 percent was in the form of grants and 58 percent was in the form of loans. The first reason for this strange contrast is that Marshall Plan aid to Western Europe was in the form of grants, not loans. A most reasonable and sensible procedure because what was at stake was the very preservation of the capitalist system on this globe; without the Marshall Plan, the United States might have become isolated

TABLE XXX
U.S. ECONOMIC AND MILITARY AID: LOANS VS. GRANTS[a]
JULY 1, 1945 TO JUNE 30, 1967

	Amount (billion $)			Percent Distribution		
	Total	Grants	Loans	Total	Grants	Loans
Developed Countries[b]	45.7	33.4	12.3	100	73	27
"Client" Countries[c]	36.9	32.0	4.9	100	87	13
All other under-developed countries	34.6	14.4	20.2	100	42	58

Footnotes and Sources: Same as Table XXIII.

as a capitalist island in a socialist sea. The second reason for the contrast is that as a rule military assistance is in the form of grants, while economic assistance, other than the Marshall Plan, is in the form of loans. This explains the heavy concentration of grants to the "client" states (a further factor is that grants to these countries also include payments for the rental of bases and communications centers).

The pattern is not much different even if we remove the influence of the Marshall Plan from our calculations. Table XXXI is the same as Table XXX, except that it covers the fiscal years 1957 to 1967, after the Marshall Plan had been completed. By this time the developed countries get much less aid;

but since the aid they do get is mainly for military purposes, the proportion in the form of grants amounts to 68 percent.

TABLE XXXI
U.S. ECONOMIC AND MILITARY AID: LOANS VS. GRANTS[a]
JULY 1, 1957 TO JUNE 30, 1967

	Amount (billion $)			Percent Distribution		
	Total	Grants	Loans	Total	Grants	Loans
Developed Countries[b]	7.5	5.1	2.4	100	68	32
"Client" Countries[c]	20.7	17.0	3.7	100	82	18
All other under-developed countries	27.8	11.1	16.7	100	40	60

Footnotes and Sources: Same as Table XXIII.

The "client" states get a somewhat smaller percentage in the form of grants than that shown in Table XXX, but it is still over 80 percent. And when we come to the bulk of the underdeveloped world, the portion of aid from the United States in the form of grants is only 40 percent, while that in the form of loans is 60 percent.

The effect of this aid-giving is that an ever larger share of the aid itself is needed merely to service past aid. On this subject, the Library of Congress report referred to above stated:

In 1964, the underdeveloped countries owed the United States over $5 billion in dollar-repayable loans, and in 1965 the amount currently due was over $500 million. On top of this, the underdeveloped countries owe over $4 billion in loans that are repayable in local currencies, rather than in dollars. The cost of maintaining such large indebtedness is at present eating up approximately 30 percent of all new assistance.[72]

This includes the debt owed by the underdeveloped countries to the United States only, and covers all the underdeveloped countries. Consider, however, what U.S. aid means to Latin America. During the years 1962 to 1966, the average annual service payments on the external public debt of all Latin America was $1,596 million. During the same years, the average annual assistance from the United States to Latin American countries, in the form of loans and grants, amounted to $1,213.[73] Thus, economic assistance from the United States did not even cover the debt service requirements of Latin America as a whole!

To appreciate what the continuous growth in debt means, an exercise in simple arithmetic is helpful. If a country borrows, say, $1,000 a year every year, before long the service payments on the debt will be larger than the inflow of money each year. An illustration of this point is given in Table XXXII. Here we take a typical loan: $1,000 is loaned to a country at 5 percent interest, to be repaid in equal instalments over 20 years. We assume further that a similar loan is made each year. As can be seen from the table, during the 5th year of such aid, almost half of the money coming in has to be used to service the past debt. In the 10th year almost 90 percent of the new money is needed for debt service. By the 15th year the capital outflow is larger than the capital inflow. In the 20th year, the borrower is paying out more than $1.50 on past debt for every $1.00 of new money he borrows.[74]

TABLE XXXII
DEBT SERVICE IF $1,000 IS BORROWED EACH YEAR: LOAN REPAID IN 20 YEARS WITH 5 PERCENT INTEREST

Year	Capital Inflow: Amount borrowed during year	Capital Outflow: Debt Service on the accumulated debt		
		Interest	Amortization	Total
5th	$1,000	$225	$250	$475
10th	1,000	388	500	888
15th	1,000	488	750	1,238
20th	1,000	525	1,000	1,525

But why should a country have to continue borrowing year after year? Won't the borrowed money be used to develop the country so that there will be enough money to pay off the debt? To answer these questions we have to appreciate the difference between an internal and an external debt. When a business man borrows internally and has to repay the debt, the procedure is very simple: as his business grows, with the help of the borrowed money, he uses his profits to repay the debt with the same kind of currency he borrowed. But if a business man or a government borrows from a foreign source, he can only repay the debt in the currency of the foreign nations. So that even if the borrowed money helps to create internal growth, the debt cannot be repaid unless there are sufficient exports to get the needed foreign currency. If exports are not sufficient to pay for the debt and buy the needed imports, then the pressure exists to make further loans. When this process comes to a head, the bankers re-schedule the loans—provided the recipient country behaves like a good boy.

And the fact is that during the postwar period the growth in service payments on the debt of the underdeveloped world has increased much more rapidly than has the growth in its exports. Hence the burden of the debt has become more oppressive and the financial dependency on the leading industrial nations and their international organizations such as the World Bank and the IMF has increased accordingly. The significance of the debt burden is highlighted in Table XXXIII. The data are shown for a selected group of countries for which estimates are available. The first column contains the percentage of each country's exports in 1966 that were used to amortize past debts. The second column presents the share of exports that were used to pay interest on their foreign debt as well as the interest and profits on foreign investment. The final column gives the total outflow of capital (debt repayment) and income as a percent of exports. What we find is that for most of the countries represented the burden of debt and payment on capital investment is at least 15 percent of exports, with quite a few in the 20 to 30 percent range.

It is especially noteworthy that this burden has been increasing throughout the postwar period. This is a reflection of (1) the more than fourfold increase in debt shown in Table XXIX and the rapid rise in foreign investment from the major capital centers, and (2) the slow rise in exports from underdeveloped countries.

The Lag in Exports

The retarded growth of exports from the underdeveloped nations shows up distinctly when contrasted with the patterns of export growth in the developed nations. This comparison is

TABLE XXXIII
PROPORTION OF EXPORTS ABSORBED BY DEBT SERVICE AND PROFITS OF FOREIGN INVESTMENT
1966

| | Percent of Exports Going to | | |
	Amortization of Public Debt	Interest on Debt and Profits on Foreign Investment	Total
Brazil	9.4[b]	13.8	23.2
Chile	10.8	19.8	30.6
Colombia	14.3[a]	18.2	32.5
Costa Rica	8.8	11.6	20.4
Ecuador	6.0	19.6	25.6[a]
Ethiopia	6.3	3.6	9.9
Guatemala	4.9	4.8[b]	9.7
Honduras	1.3	9.0[b]	10.3
India	11.9	15.6[n]	26.9
Kenya	4.3	12.1[b]	16.4
Mexico	29.3	30.4	59.7
Nicaragua	4.8	11.6	16.4
Nigeria	4.5	26.2	30.7
Pakistan	6.4[b]	9.3	15.7
Panama	3.3	10.1	13.4
Paraguay	5.1	8.2	13.3
Peru	4.8	15.5	20.3
Philippines	7.2	5.1	12.3
Turkey	3.5	20.3[c]	23.8
Uruguay	9.0[b]	8.1[b]	17.1
Venezuela	1.2[b]	24.9	26.1

(a) 1961.
(b) 1965.
(c) Does not include profit on foreign investment.
Source: Calculated from data, as follows: Amortization of Debt from same source as in Table XXXII; Interest on Debt and Profits on foreign investment from United Nations, *The External Financing of Economic Development, International flow of long-term capital and official donations, 1962-1966,* New York, 1968, Table 29; Exports from International Monetary Fund, *Direction of Trade Annual 1962-1966,* Washington, D. C. (no date). (The amortization data for Brazil are from the United Nations source cited.)

made in Table XXXIV. During the fifteen years from 1950 to 1965, exports from developed countries grew at an annual rate of 8.5 percent. Such a rapid rise gives a decided advantage to the developed countries: it provides them with the foreign ex-

TABLE XXXIV
PATTERNS OF EXPORT GROWTH:
DEVELOPED VS. UNDERDEVELOPED COUNTRIES

	Value of Exports (Billions of $)		Annual Rate of Growth
	1950	1965	1950 to 1965
World Exports, total	53.5	156.3	7.4%
Exports of Developed Countries, total	35.9	122.5	8.5%
To Each Other	25.0	95.5	9.4%
To Underdeveloped Countries	10.9	27.0	6.2%
Exports of Underdeveloped Countries, total	17.6	33.8	4.5%
To Developed Countries	12.4	26.2	5.2%
To Each Other	5.2	7.6	2.5%
Exports of underdeveloped Countries, excluding major petroleum producers, total	14.2	23.7	3.6%
To Developed Countries	10.0	18.5	4.2%
To Each Other	4.1	5.2	1.7%

Source: Hal B. Lary, *Imports of Manufactures from Less Developed Countries,* New York, 1968, p. 2.

change to pay a rapid increase in imports, to service their external debt, and to export capital as well. The decidedly slower growth rate of the exports of the underdeveloped countries (4.5 percent per year) provides insufficient means to keep pace with the payments that have to be made on the burgeoning debt and for the profits repatriated by foreign investors. This is especially so for the non-oil-exporting countries where the anual rate of growth in exports is only 3.6 percent per year.

The underlying reasons for these differences in export growth can be traced to the variations in the growth of demand for (1) food and raw materials, the major exports of the underdeveloped world, and (2) manufactures, the major exports of the developed nations. As can be seen from Table XXXV, world trade of the former items increased two thirds from 1938 to

1963; for the latter, world trade went up more than 250 percent. The same divergent patterns are evident also since 1963. Only

TABLE XXXV
PATTERNS OF EXPORT GROWTH BY TYPE OF PRODUCT

Volume of World Exports
(1963 = 100)

	Food and Raw Materials	Fuel	Manufactured Goods
1938	61	29	28
1953	62	52	50
1960	89	78	82
1963	100	100	100
1966	113	127	136

Source: United Nations, *Statistical Yearbook 1967*, New York, 1968.

the exports of the oil-producing countries have kept pace with the trends of manufactured goods exports. However, the buoyant export trade for most of these countries has meant an unusually large outflow of profits to foreign owners of the oil fields.

The contrasting situation in the demand for food and many types of raw materials, on the one hand, and for manufactures, on the other hand, is reflected in differences in the price trends of these categories: many of the food and raw materials producers have been in a buyers' market, while many of the manufacturers have been in a sellers' market. This means of course that the prices of exports of food and raw materials have deteriorated relative to the prices of manufactures—a trend compounded by the high degree of monopoly in the manufacturing centers. In other words, the terms of trade—the relation of prices which countries pay for imports to the prices they receive for exports—have been adverse for the underdeveloped countries.

The significance of this development has been intensively studied by United Nations economists. A summary result of their studies is shown in Table XXXVI. The first column provides a measure of the estimated losses in purchasing power experienced by the underdeveloped countries as a result of the adverse terms of trade since 1953 to 1957. The comparison of this loss in purchasing power with aid flowing from the developed countries (shown in the last column) shows that an important proportion of the aid flowing from the developing countries was absorbed by the losses due to the adverse trend in the terms of trade. If we correlate this development with the phenomenon of rising debt, we find the following: (a) an increasing proportion of the exports of the underdeveloped countries has to be used for servicing the debt, and (b) the decreasing proportion of exports available for normal imports or for economic growth has been effectively contracted further because of the loss in purchasing power of the exports.

TABLE XXXVI
LOSS IN PURCHASING POWER OF EXPORTS FROM UNDERDEVELOPED COUNTRIES

	Losses Due to Decline in Terms of Trade[a]	Economic Aid from Developed Countries[b]	Losses as Percent of Official aid
	(Millions of $)		
1961	—1,824	4,996	36.5%
1962	—2,158	5,390	40.0
1963	—2,109	5,914	35.7
1964	—2,026	5,947	34.1
1965	—2,519	6,203	40.1
1966	—2,752	6,430[c]	42.8
Total	—13,388	34,880	38.4%

(a) This represents an estimate of the net losses in purchasing power experienced by underdeveloped countries because of changes in terms of trade. The calculation is based on the average prices received for exports and paid for imports during the period 1953-1957.
(b) Financial flows from non-Communist governments and multilateral organizations (e.g., World Bank).
(c) Estimated.
Source: United Nations Conference on Trade and Development, Review of International Trade and Development, 1967 (Document TD/5, November 15, 1967, prepared for Second Session, New Delhi, India, February 1, 1968), pp. 35-36.

The Limits on Exports

A 1965 article in *The Economist* (London) summarizes the lagging trend of Latin American exports and the reasons for it in these terms:

Rough interpolations from estimates by the United Nations' admirable Economic Commission for Latin America suggest that if the index figure of the external purchasing power of Latin America's exports per head (excluding oil-rich Venezuela) is taken as 100 in 1928, it was down to 37 by 1955 and is probably about 32 now. This failure of exports to expand in line with rising population has come about partly because of a relative sluggishness of international demand for primary products compared with manufactured products, partly because of the appearance of alternative sources of supply in Africa and elsewhere, but more generally because the whole international trading and monetary system is riveted in a form which hampers countries that had become committed to one sort of exporting structure from moving easily into another sort of exporting structure, even if they are sensibly changing their internal productive systems at the same time. Most of this whole area of Latin America, which had been encouraged by the world trading system of the late nineteenth and early twentieth century to become the most export-intensive area on earth, has therefore never really had a chance of escaping into affluence, during an appalling period of blight in which it has seen two thirds of the real *per capita* value of its exports cut away.[75]

The economic and political processes of the industrial nations act as a barrier to the export expansion of the underdeveloped countries and thereby, willy-nilly, continuously reimpose economic-financial dependency on the latter. We will here mention only two aspects of this: (1) the influence of U.S. foreign investment, and (2) the restrictions imposed by U.S. tariff walls.

The real hope for developing larger export markets and thereby getting out of the debt bind lies in exports of manufactured goods. This is the buoyant area in international trade. However, the best and most fruitful spheres of manufacturing activity are usually taken over by foreign investors. These investors with multinational interests, producing in many areas of the globe, are not interested in exporting to other nations from their investments in the underdeveloped countries, for the simple reason that they are not interested in competing with themselves.

Thus, look at the difference between the export pattern of U.S.-owned mining firms in Latin America, shown in Table XXXVII, and that of U.S.-owned manufacturing firms in Latin America, shown in Table XXXVIII. U.S. mining firms in for-

TABLE XXXVII

SALES OF U.S.-OWNED MINING FIRMS IN LATIN AMERICA
1965

| | Sales (Million $) | | | | Percent of Total | | | |
	Total	Local Sales	Exported to U.S.	Exported to Other Countries	Total	Local Sales	Exported to U.S.	Exported to Other Countries
Latin America, Total	1,345	240	535	570	100.0	17.8	39.8	42.4
Mexico, Central America, and West Indies	270	126	94	50	100.0	46.7	34.8	18.5
South America	915	114	301	500	100.0	12.5	32.9	54.6
Other Western Hemisphere	160	—	140	20	100.0	—	87.5	12.5

Source: *Survey of Current Business*, November 1966.

eign countries are operated (a) to supply the raw materials needs of U.S. firms located in the United States and elsewhere, and (b) to secure a large enough share of world production so that prices and production can be regulated to maximize profits. This naturally has two significant results: (1) the bulk of the production is exported (82 percent for all of Latin America), and (2) the price and production policies of these firms are governed by the profit goals of the U.S. owners and not by the balance-of-payments needs of these countries or their requirements for foreign exchange to pay for capital imports. There is one additional aspect that needs to be mentioned. Except for oil, the demand for minerals in the advanced countries has not been keeping pace with the demand for manufactured goods. As has been mentioned earlier, this does not mean a lessening of the importance of these raw materials; what it does mean is that increasing efficiency in the use of raw materials depresses the export potential of the countries relying on such exports for their livelihood.

Now let us look at the export patterns of U.S.-owned manufacturing plants in the flourishing international markets for manufactured goods. As can be seen from Table XXXVIII, less than 8 percent of the output of U.S. firms in Latin America goes into the export trade. The only group for which exports are significant is food, and this is usually an extension of the extraction of natural resources, representing the processing of agricultural products (for example, processed oil, seeds, coffee, meat, and leather). In two other natural-resource product groups—paper and chemicals—the percentage of exports is above the average, but still small considering the needs of these countries for foreign exchange to service their debt, let alone provide for growth. When we come to the other groups, the export percentage is less than 6 percent; in the rubber, electrical machinery, and transportation equipment groups, less than 4 percent goes to export markets.

The explanation of this pattern is spelled out, with particular reference to Brazil, in an article in Harvard University's *Quarterly Journal of Economics*:

Another institutional barrier to exports has been introduced by

TABLE XXXVIII

SALES OF U.S.-OWNED MANUFACTURING FIRMS IN LATIN AMERICA
1965

	Sales (Million $)				Percent of Total			
Industry	Total	Local Sales	Exported to U.S.	Exported to Other Countries	Total	Local Sales	Exported to U.S.	Exported to Other Countries
Food Products	867	674	46	147	100.0	77.7	5.3	17.0
Paper and Allied products	178	158	5	15	100.0	88.8	2.8	8.4
Chemicals	1,398	1,260	34	104	100.0	90.1	2.4	7.5
Rubber Products	350	348	—	2	100.0	99.3	—	0.6
Primary and Fabricated Metals	309	297	—	12	100.0	96.1	—	3.9
Machinery, except Electrical	242	227	2	13	100.0	93.8	0.8	5.4
Electrical Machinery	392	386	1	5	100.0	98.5	0.2	1.3
Transportation Equipment	1,172	1,164	3	5	100.0	99.3	0.3	0.4
Other Products	576	559	10	7	100.0	97.1	1.7	1.2
Total	5,484	5,073	101	310	100.0	92.5	1.8	5.7

Source: *Survey of Current Business*, November 1966.

the fact that a good portion of Brazilian manufacturing output, and particularly of the more efficient companies, is produced by firms which are either subsidiaries of foreign companies or work under licenses from foreign companies. The foreign companies have often barred these Brazilian firms from competing with them either in their home markets or in third countries.[76]

The other side of this coin is that when Brazilian manufacturers take the initiative to develop an industry that processes home-grown products and thereby competes with U.S. firms, they get slapped down by the whole weight of U.S. influence and control. Brazil began to make powdered coffee from cheap broken beans which are not offered on the world market. In this way, Brazil, in the past three years, took over about 11 percent of the U.S. instant-coffee market. This became a major area of dispute as the United States began to protest against "unfair competition." Despite all the good-will for the anti-Goulart regime, the United States could not neglect the interest of its own coffee manufacurers. The result was that Brazil was forced to accept an agreement whereby, in the words of *The Economist,* Brazilian manufacturers of instant coffee

must produce under conditions "comparable" to those of the big American manufacturers who buy Brazilian beans for processing. Brazil, in other words, is to get very little advantage from the fact that it is the world's biggest coffee grower and has been saddled with vast stocks for decades, beyond the fact that the American processors will have to pay higher transport costs . . . the [Brazilian] government has now undertaken to impose an export tax on Brazilian powdered coffee which will, in effect, make the broken beans sold by the government as dear to its own exporters of instant coffee as the good beans are to the American processors. Brazil was forced to accept the settlement partly because of the heavy pressure that the Americans brought to bear (it is rumored that they threatened—diplomatically of course—to cut Brazil's aid allocation) but also because Brazil's position within the International Coffee Agreement is weak.[77]

But it is not only the heavy hand of direct intervention that tips the balance in favor of U.S. business in its relations with the underdeveloped countries. The very structure of the U.S. tariff system is designed to cut off the large U.S. market from the direct competition that might arise from the underdeveloped countries.

The general tariff practice in the United States is to admit, free of customs, imports of raw materials that are either not produced in this country or are in relatively short supply. As soon as any processing is done on these raw materials, such as sawing a log or taking pits out of dates, a tariff is imposed to restrict imports. As analyzed by a Committee for Economic Development study, ". . . even moderate tariffs on materials that have been through the early stage of processing often result in a high degree of effective protection for the processing industry itself. This is because the tariff is levied on the total value of the processed product but the value added in the processing industries is only a small percentage of this total value."[78] The same study proceeds to illustrate why this is so:

For example, suppose that the world price of a certain type of leather is $100 and the cost of the hides to make the leather is $70. Then the "value added" is $30. Now assume that imports of hides . . . are duty-free, but the imports of leather are subject to a 10 percent tariff. The tanner . . . is, therefore, in a position to charge $110 for the leather. But the $10 duty protects not the cost of producing hides, which can be imported free of duty, but only the "value added" in tanning the hides which amounts to $30. Thus, a nominal tariff of 10 percent on leather gives effective protection to the tanning industry equivalent to 33⅓ percent by permitting the domestic producer to incur higher costs to that extent on his processing operation.[79]

The walls erected against imports of the processed natural resources of underdeveloped countries can be appreciated from merely a few illustrations of the customs duties in effect in 1968:[80]

Bananas. Whole fresh bananas come into the United States free of duty. If they are dried before being shipped to the United States, there is a 6½ percent ad valorem duty. (Ad valorem is the price shown on the shipper's invoice.) Should the bananas be otherwise prepared or preserved, there is a 13 percent ad valorem duty.

Tobacco. Tobacco stems that are not cut, ground or pulverized come in duty free. If they are cut, ground or pulverized, there is a 55 cents per pound duty.

Cocoa. Cocoa beans come in free. On cocoa butter there is a 5½ percent ad valorem duty. On sweetened cocoa there is a 9 percent duty, and on candy containing cocoa the duty goes up to 12½ percent.

Dates. Dates packed in units over 10 pounds command a duty of only 1 cent per pound. However, if the dates come in smaller packages, the duty comes to 7½ cents per pound. Even on the larger packages, if the shipper arranges to have the pits removed, the duty goes up from 1 cent to 2 cents per pound. On dates otherwise prepared or preserved, there is a 35 percent duty.

Iron and steel. Iron ore comes in free of duty. If the iron ore has been converted to pig iron, a duty of 16 cents per ton is imposed. Further processing brings higher duties. For example, 5 cents per pound has to be paid on imports of bars of wrought iron. Cast iron pipes or tubes carry a 10 percent ad valorem duty, while dressmaker or common pins require a 20 percent tariff. On hooks and eyes, the duty is 3.3 cents per pound plus 18.5 percent ad valorem.

Copper. The same pattern is observable in copper, as in other minerals and metals. Copper-bearing ores come in free of duty. For copper powders, the duty is 1.1 cents per pound plus 15.5 percent ad valorem. For pipes and tubes, seamless, the importer pays 4.5 cents per pound. For thumbtacks made of copper, the duty is 14 percent ad valorem.

Lumber. Logs and timber in the rough, even logs that are split and hewn, carry no duty. But even rough lumber has to climb over the tariff walls, from 28 cents per 1,000 feet (board measure) for spruce to 80 cents per 1,000 feet for douglas fir, hemlock, and larch. If the lumber is converted into broom and mop handles, there is a 7.5 percent ad valorem duty. On toothpicks, the duty climbs to 11 percent.

The energetic protection of domestic business by tariffs, quotas and special treaties is an essential element of U.S. international economic policy. The tariff walls protect the prosperity and safety of U.S. business and improve the living standards of those inside the wall. However, such a wall around the largest single market in the capitalist world is a major inhibitor of the growth potential of those nations confined to being the suppliers of food and raw materials; it also contributes substantially to the perpetuation of the debtor status of the natural-resource-supplying nations.

Summary

The term imperialism is commonly restricted to the acquisition of colonies and/or the political and military actions of a government to protect the foreign investments of its citizens. Viewed in this fashion, the concept of imperialism is restricted to a narrow group of practices and policies. Such practices and policies, however, are merely special cases of a much more complex reality in which there is a general intertwining of trade and flag. In effect, there is in the United States, as in other imperialist centers, an underlying unity of the domestic economy, the foreign economic activity of industry and finance, the military, and international diplomacy.

This unity flows from the normal functioning of a capitalist economy, and becomes especially pronounced and pervasive when there is a high degree of concentration of economic power in the major industrial and financial sectors of the economy. Concentration of economic power can be achieved, maintained, and increased when the wielders of this power can substantially control the environment in which they operate. This control is necessary for the safety of the capital invested and as an important source of increased profits. The imperatives of control and profit growth involve extensions of economic activity beyond national borders: to control and influence raw materials sources, to control and influence markets, and to obtain higher profit rates through cheaper labor and other inputs.

The striving for control involves conflicts between giant corporations within a country. But more important is the economic conflict among the economic giants of the chief industrialized nations. This conflict, actual and potential, intensifies the pressure to attain control over raw material sources and international markets. Only in this way can existing competition be defeated and new competitors be shut out.

In all this, finance acts as a necessary and useful partner. On the one hand, the drive for control by industry is stimulated and supported by the international expansion and strength of financial institutions. On the other hand, the international expansion of finance finds support and opportunity in the international operations of business. Which comes first is not especially significant. The economics of competitive industry and of competitive banking both lead to concentration of power and the search for control in domestic and foreign operations. In this process, conflicts of interest may arise between specific industrial-financial groups and various alliances may be formed. But the process itself is such that each—industry and finance—feeds on the success of the other.

A necessary condition for this type of economic growth is a sympathetic political and military environment: international political and military activity and alliances must be directed to establishing and sustaining political and military control and influence. Here, too, the issue is not which comes first. Economic control, military control, and political control mutually support and stimulate each other.

A new high in this kind of interrelationship has been reached by the United States in the post-Second-World-War world. Circumstances and the striving of U.S. economic, political, and military activity have led to a situation in which U.S. institutions can dominate the capitalist world. In the absence of a reshuffle of power among the imperialist interests or a change in the balance of power between the imperialist and non-imperialist worlds, the United States can call the tune as the main protector and organizer of the imperialist network.

The great prosperity of the United States during the postwar years is rooted in this dominating role. The maintenance of the military establishment and its activities has been a major source of direct and indirect business activity and profits. Industry and finance profitably expanded abroad under the protection of this globe-striding military force. The military, financial, and industrial foreign expansion supported the U.S. assumption of world banking leadership and the domination of the dollar as a world currency. In turn, the central role of the U.S. money market has been instrumental in financing military operations abroad, the international expansion of industry and banking, and the use of foreign aid as a means of controlling and dominating the imperialist network.

NOTES

1. "Defense Programs and the Balance of Payments," in Joint Economic Committee of the Congress of the United States, *The United States Balance of Payments—Perspectives and Policies*, Washington, D.C.,

1963, Part III, p. 77. This part of the report was prepared by the Department of Defense.

2. Address by Secretary of Defense Robert S. McNamara before the American Society of Newspaper Editors, Montreal, Canada, *The New York Times*, May 19, 1966.

3. Address by President Kennedy before the Economic Club, New York City, December 1962, as quoted in Committee on Foreign Relations, U.S. Senate, *Some Important Issues in Foreign Aid* (A report prepared by the Legislative Reference Service of the Library of Congress), Washington, D.C., 1966, p. 15.

4. The President's Committee to Strengthen the Security of the Free World, *The Scope and Distribution of United States Military and Economic Assistance Programs,* Washington, D.C., March 1963, as reprinted in David Baldwin, *Foreign Aid and American Foreign Policy,* New York, 1966, p. 242.

5. Joan M. Nelson, *Aid, Influence, and Foreign Policy,* New York, 1968, p. 11.

6. Department of State and Department of Defense, *The Mutual Security Program Fiscal Year 1958,* Washington, D.C., June 1957, p. 106.

7. Halford L. Hoskins, "Aid and Diplomacy in the Middle East," *Current History,* July 1966, p. 15.

8. John D. Montgomery, *Foreign Aid in International Politics,* Englewood Cliffs, New Jersey, 1967, p. 17.

9. *The New York Times,* July 14, 1968.

10. *The Economist,* February 3, 1968, p. 23.

11. *The New York Times,* January 24, 1966.

12. *Ibid.,* February 22, 1966.

13. *Ibid.,* September 14, 1966.

14. *Ibid.,* September 16, 1966.

15. *The Economist,* February 19, 1966, p. 791.

16. Testimony of Secretary of Defense Robert S. McNamara at Committee on Foreign Affairs, House of Representatives, *Hearings on the Foreign Assistance Act of 1967,* Washington, D.C., 1967, p. 114.

17. *Ibid.,* pp. 116-117.

18. *Ibid.,* p. 117.

19. Subcommittee of the Committee on Appropriations, House of Representatives, 87th Congress, 2nd Session. *Hearings,* Washington, D.C., 1962, Vol. I, p. 359.

20. *Congressional Record,* May 24, 1965, p. 10840, as quoted in report cited in footnote 3.

21. Same *Hearings* as cited in footnote 16, p. 538. Such aversion to violence naturally does not extend to actions by military forces, trained and financed by the United States, to overthrow an elected government, or to prevent an election, as most recently in Greece, where it is anticipated that the majority of the electorate will support a government which does not suit the local military officers or the United States.

22. Same Report as cited in footnote 3, p. 19.

23. *Ibid.,* p. 32.

24. Joan M. Nelson, *op. cit.,* p. 112.

25. Committee on Foreign Affairs, House of Representatives, *Report on Foreign Policy and Mutual Security Program*, Washington, D.C., 1957, p. 39.

26. See Article VII of the Anglo-American Financial Agreement as cited in footnote 39, p. 112.

27. *The Economist*, May 28, 1967.

28. Herbert Feldman, "Aid as Imperialism?", *International Affairs*, April 1967, p. 229.

29. *The New York Times*, February 3, 1953.

30. Republic of the Philippines, *Treaty Series*, Vol. II, No. 4, April 1956. Note the reference in the treaty to "mineral lands of the public domain." Philippine law follows the Spanish rather than the Anglo-Saxon tradition on mineral rights. This means that in the Philippines minerals in the subsoil are in the public domain and do not belong to the private owner of the land. Hence, the equal treatment for Philippine and U.S. citizens amounts to (a) equal opportunity for U.S. business firms to develop mines in all the Philippine subsoil, and (b) equal opportunity for Philippine business firms to exploit U.S. land in the public domain—as, for example, Yellowstone Park.

31. *Foreign Assistance Act of 1963, 77 Stat. 388*, as quoted in Marina von Neumann Whitman, *Government Risk-Sharing in Foreign Investment*, Princeton, New Jersey, 1965, p. 114.

32. Committee on Foreign Relations, U.S. Senate *Hearings on Foreign Assistance Act of 1962*, Washington, D.C., 1962, p. 27.

33. Joan M. Nelson, *op. cit.*, pp. 107-8.

34. *Forbes Magazine*, March 1, 1966.

35. Statement of Joseph Palmer, II, Assistant Secretary of State for African Affairs in Committee on Foreign Affairs, House of Representatives, *Hearings on Foreign Assistance Act of 1968*, Washington, D.C., 1968, Part II, p. 326.

36. From an address delivered at the National Foreign Trade Convention, New York, November 18, 1964, as quoted in Charles D. Hyson and Alan M. Strout, "Impact of Foreign Aid on U.S. Exports," *Harvard Business Review*, January-February 1968, p. 63.

37. Dr. Mahbub Ul Haq, of the Pakistan Planning Commission, "Tied Credits—A Quantitative Analysis," in J. H. Adler, ed., *Capital Movements*, London, 1967, p. 330.

38. Article referred to in footnote 36, p. 69.

39. Edward S. Mason, *Foreign Aid and Foreign Policy*, New York, 1964, p. 14.

40. J. N. Behrman, "Foreign Investment and the Transfer of Knowledge and Skills," in Raymond F. Mikesell, ed., *U.S. Private and Government Investment Abroad*, Eugene, Oregon, 1962, p. 132.

41. Eugene R. Black, "The Domestic Dividends of Foreign Aid," *Columbia Journal of World Business*, Fall 1965, p. 25.

42. John D. Montgomery, *Foreign Aid in International Politics*, Englewood Cliffs, New Jersey, 1967, p. 20. The quotation is from a *New York Times* item, September 18, 1963.

43. Same *Hearings* as in footnote 35, Part II, p. 296.

44. Same *Hearings* as in footnote 16, p. 1263.

45. Economic Research Service, U.S. Department of Agriculture, *12 Years of Achievement under Public Law 480*, Washington, D.C., November 1967, p. 8.

46. *The New York Times*, December 5, 1965.

47. Committee on Foreign Affairs, *Hearings on Foreign Assistance Act of 1966*, Washington, D.C., 1966, pp. 520-521.

48. As quoted in A. P. Thornton, *The Imperial Idea and Its Enemies*, London, 1959, pp. 357-358.

49. Jacob J. Kaplan, *The Challenge of Foreign Aid*, N.Y., 1967, p. 213.

50. *Ibid.*, pp. 208-209.

51. Sec. 647.22 U.S.C. 2406, Public Law 87-195, Part 3.

52. Agency for International Development, *Proposed Economic Assistance Programs FY 1967*, Washington, D.C., March 1966, p. 75.

53. *Ibid.*, p. 79.

54. Testimony of William S. Gaud, Administrator, Agency for International Development, as reported in Committee on Foreign Affairs, House of Representatives, *Hearings on Foreign Assistance Act of 1968*, pp. 184-185.

55. Norman D. Palmer, *South Asia and United States Policy*, Boston, Mass., 1956, p. 156. The reference within this quotation is to John P. Lewis, *Quiet Crisis in India*, Washington, D.C., 1962.

56. Dr. Christoph Beringer and Irshad Ahmad, *The Use of Agricultural Surplus Commodities for Economic Development in Pakistan*, Karachi, January 1964, p. 14.

57. Sa'id El-Naggar, *Foreign Aid and the Economic Development of the United Arab Republic* (Princeton Near East Papers No. 1), Princeton, New Jersey, 1965.

58. Agency for International Development, *Principles of Foreign Economic Assistance*, Washington, D.C., September 1965, p. 47. Note that the term "developing countries" in this and other quotations is a euphemism for underdeveloped countries.

59. Edward S. Mason, *op. cit.*, pp. 47-48.

60. Committee on Foreign Relations, U.S. Senate, *Survey of the Alliance for Progress—Inflation in Latin America*, Washington, D.C., September 25, 1967, p. 38 footnote.

61. See Columbia University School of Law, *Public International Development Financing in Thailand* (Report No. 4), New York, February 1963, pp. 81-83.

62. David A. Baldwin, *Economic Development and American Foreign Policy, 1943-1962*, Chicago, 1966, p. 36.

63. Raymond F. Mikesell, "Problems and Policies in Public Lending for Economic Development," in Raymond F. Mikesell, ed., *op. cit.*, pp. 358-359.

64. *The New York Times*, April 23, 1959.

65. Thomas Balogh, *The Economics of Poverty*, London, 1966, pp. 28-29. Readers interested in economic theory and the problems of underdeveloped countries will be rewarded by studying Chapter 1 of this book, "Economic Policy and the Price System."

66. An IMF publication describes in general terms the requirements imposed by the Fund when stabilization loans are made: "They include also undertakings or declarations of intention regarding other aspects

of international good behavior, such as the adoption of sound domestic financial policies and the limitation of trade restrictions. It has been found in practice that, unless countries hold in check any inflationary tendencies they may be experiencing, they can neither repay their drawings from the Fund within due time nor progress toward the achievement of Fund objectives, such as exchange stability and the removal of restrictions on current international transactions. Therefore, drawings and stand-by arrangements are often made conditional upon the adoption of programs of financial stabilization, including rather precise undertakings with respect to public finance, quantitative limitations on central bank expansion, minimum reserve requirements for commercial banks, etc." J. Marcus Fleming, *The International Monetary Fund, Its Form and Functioning*, Washington, D.C., 1964, pp. 35-36. For a careful study of the consequences of IMF control conditions in Argentina, see Eprime Eshag and Rosemary Thorp, "Economic and Social Consequences of Orthodox Economic Policies in Argentina in the Post-War Years," *Bulletin of the Oxford University Institute of Economics and Statistics*, February 1965.

67. Joan M. Nelson, *op. cit.*, p. 83.
68. Raymond F. Mikesell, ed., *op. cit.*, p. 356.
69. *The New York Times*, August 25, 1967.
70. Exports from underdeveloped countries to non-Communist countries in 1956 were $24.1 billion; in 1966, $35.7 billion. Source: United Nations, *Statistical Yearbook*, 1967, New York, 1968.
71. Outflow of assistance from developed countries to underdeveloped countries mounted to $9.1 billion in 1966. United Nations, *The External Financing of Economic Development, International Flow of Long-Term Capital and Official Donations, 1962-1966*, New York, 1968, Table 3.
72. Same as Report cited in footnote 3, p. 69.
73. Service payments calculated from source cited in Table XXIX. U.S. aid figure is from Council of Economic Advisers, *Annual Report 1968*, Table B-86.
74. For the mathematics of these and other assumptions, see Goran Ohlin, *Aid and Indebtedness*, Paris, 1966.
75. "No Christ on the Andes," *The Economist*, September 25, 1965, p. x.
76. Nathaniel H. Leff, "Export Stagnation and Autarkic Development in Brazil, 1947-1962," in *Quarterly Journal of Economics*, May 1967, p. 291.
77. *The Economist*, February 24, 1968, p. 72.
78. Committee for Economic Development, *Trade Policy Toward Low-Income Countries*, New York, June 1967, p. 20.
79. *Ibid.*, p. 20.
80. The duties cited are from U.S. Tariff Commission, *Tariff Schedule of the United States Annotated (1968)*, Washington, D.C., 1967. For additional illustrations, as well as other valuable information and analysis, see Jacob Oser, *Promoting Economic Development, with Illustrations from Kenya*, Evanston, Illinois, 1967.

5

THE AMERICAN EMPIRE
AND THE U. S. ECONOMY

Three interrelated views on economic imperialism and United States foreign policy prevail today:

(1) Economic imperialism *is not* at the root of United States foreign policy. Instead, political aims and national security are the prime motivators of foreign policy.

(2) Economic imperialism *cannot* be the main element in foreign policy determination, since United States foreign trade and foreign investment make such relatively small contributions to the nation's overall economic performance.

(3) Since foreign economic involvement is relatively unimportant to the United States economy, it follows that economic imperialism *need not* be a motivating force in foreign policy. Hence some liberal and left critics argue that present foreign policy, to the extent that it is influenced by imperialism, is misguided and in conflict with the best economic interests of this country. If we sincerely encouraged social and economic development abroad, the argument goes, even to the extent of financing the nationalization of United States foreign investment, the rising demand for capital imports by underdeveloped countries would create a more substantial and lasting stimulus to prosperity than the current volume of foreign trade and foreign investment.

Obscuring economic and commercial interests by covering them up or intermingling them with idealistic and religious motivations is hardly a new phenomenon. Wars have been fought to impose Christianity on heathen empires—wars which incidentally also opened up new trade routes or established new centers of commercial monopoly. Even such a crass commercial aggression as the Opium War in China was explained to the United States public by the American Board of Commissioners for Foreign Missions as "not so much an opium or an English affair, as the result of a great design of Providence to make the wickedness of men subserve his purposes of mercy toward China, in breaking through her wall of exclusion, and bringing the empire into more immediate contact with Western and Christian nations."[1]

John Quincy Adams, in a public lecture on the Opium War, explained that China's trade policy was contrary to the law of nature and Christian principles:

> The moral obligation of commercial intercourse between nations is founded entirely, exclusively, upon the Christian precept to love your neighbor as yourself. . . . But China, not being a Christian nation, its inhabitants do not consider themselves bound by the Christian precept, to love their neighbor as themselves. . . . This is a churlish and unsocial system. . . . The fundamental principle of the Chinese Empire is anti-commercial. . . . It admits no obligation to hold commercial intercourse with others. . . . It is time that this enormous outrage upon the rights of human nature, and upon the first principles of the rights of nations, should cease.[2]

Perhaps the Christian principle of "love thy neighbor" and the more modern ethic that the anti-commercial is also immoral have become so habitual in accepted ways of thought that we have lost the facility to separate the various strands that make up foreign policy. Perhaps the source of the difficulty can be traced to a lack of understanding of what Bernard Baruch called "the essential one-ness of [United States] economic, political and strategic interests."[3]

There will probably be little dispute about the "one-ness" of United States political and national security aims. The only rationale of national security today is "defense" against the Soviet Union and China. To be absolutely safe, it is said, we need also to cope with the "concealed wars" which may appear as internal revolutions or civil war.[4] It is merely coincidental, to be sure, that socialist revolutions destroy the institutions of private ownership of the means of production and thereby violate the Christian precept to love thy neighbor by eliminating freedom of trade and freedom of enterprise in large and important sectors of the earth.

The "one-ness" of the political and national security aims becomes more evident on examination of the political aims, since in this realm of thought our policy-makers and policy-defenders are strict economic determinists. Political freedom is equated with Western-style democracy. The economic basis of this democracy is free enterprise. Hence the political aim of defense of the free world must also involve the defense of free trade and free enterprise. The primary departure from this rigid economic determinism appears when dealing with politically unstable nations where, obviously, the art of self-government is not fully developed. In such cases, for the sake of political stability, we permit and encourage military dictatorships, in full confidence that the people of these countries will eventually learn the art of self-government and adopt a free society just so long as the proper underpinning of free enterprise remains.

While our policy-makers and policy-defenders will identify in the most general terms the "one-ness" of the nation's foreign political and national security goals, they usually become quite shy when it comes to the question of the unity of these goals and economic interests. We have come a long way from the very straightforward bulletin prepared in 1922 by the Office of Naval Intelligence on "The U.S. Navy as an Industrial Asset."[5] This report frankly details the services rendered by the Navy in protecting American business interests and in seeking out commercial and investment opportunities which the Navy Department brings to the attention of American businessmen.

But today our national aims are presumably concerned only with political and philosophic ideals. In so far as economic interests are concerned, the tables have been turned: today it is business that is expected to serve the needs of national policy. The problem is how to stimulate private investment abroad. Private foreign investment is considered such a necessary tool of national policy that various forms of investment guaranty programs have been designed to protect foreign investors against losses due to confiscation, wars, and the uncertainties of currency convertibility.

The interrelation between economic interests and foreign policy is seen more clearly by business-minded observers. Thus the former president and chairman of the World Bank, Eugene R. Black, informs us that "our foreign aid programs constitute a distinct benefit to American business. The three major benefits are: (1) Foreign aid provides a substantial and immediate market for U.S. goods and services. (2) Foreign aid stimulates the development of new overseas markets for U.S. companies. (3) Foreign aid orients national economies toward a free enterprise system in which U.S. firms can prosper."[6]

More specifically, an Assistant Secretary of Commerce for Economic Affairs explains to businessmen that "if these [military and economic] aid programs were discontinued, private investments might be a waste because it would not be safe enough for you to make them."[7]

On a much more elevated plane, we are told by a specialist on international business practice, a teacher at MIT and Harvard: "It would seem that there is a horrible urgency in making Western economic concepts internationally viable if man's dignity is to be preserved—and incidentally, a profitable private business."[8]

And as an indication of how in fact some influential members of the business community see the "one-ness" of economic, political, and security interests, listen to the view expressed in 1965 by the Vice-President of Chase Manhattan Bank who supervises Far Eastern operations:

In the past, foreign investors have been somewhat wary of the over-all political prospect for the [Southeast Asia] region. I must say, though, that the U.S. actions in Vietnam this year— which have demonstrated that the U.S. will continue to give effective protection to the free nations of the region—have considerably reassured both Asian and Western investors. In fact, I see some reason for hope that the same sort of economic growth may take place in the free economies of Asia that took place in Europe after the Truman Doctrine and after NATO provided a protective shield. The same thing also took place in Japan after the U.S. intervention in Korea removed investor doubts.[9]

The Size of Foreign Economic Involvement

But even if we grant the interrelatedness of economic, political, and security interests, how much priority should we assign to economic interests? Specifically, how can one claim that economic imperialism plays a *major* role in United States policy if total exports are less than 5 percent of the gross national product, and foreign investment much less than 10 percent of domestic capital investment?

Let us note first that the size of ratios is not by itself an adequate indicator of what motivates foreign policy. Many wars and military operations were aimed at control over China's markets at a time when those markets represented only one percent of total world trade. Overall percentages need analytical examination: the strategic and policy-influential areas of business activity need to be sorted out.

Above all, it is important to appreciate that the stake of United States business abroad is many times larger than the volume of merchandise exports. The reason for this is that the volume of accumulated capital abroad controlled by United States business has been increasing at a faster rate than exports. The unique advantage of capital is that it reproduces itself. That is, the output obtained by capital investment produces enough revenue to cover not only costs of labor and raw materials but also the capital and natural resources consumed plus profits. The annual flow of capital invested abroad is therefore additive: increments to capital enlarge the productive base. Even more important, United States firms abroad are able to mobilize foreign capital for their operations. The net result of the flow of capital abroad and the foreign capital mobilized by American firms is that while production abroad arising out of United States investment was $4\frac{1}{2}$ times larger than exports in 1950, by 1964 this had risen to $5\frac{1}{2}$ times exports. These observations are based on estimates made in a recent study conducted by the National Industrial Conference Board[10] (see table top of following page).

When the Department of Commerce measures the economic significance of exports, it compares them with a figure for total domestic production of moveable goods—that is, the

	Sales (in Billions)	
	1950	1964
Output abroad resulting from U.S. investment		
From direct investment*	$24	$ 88
From other investment**	20	55
Total	44	143
Sales abroad via exports	10	25
Total output abroad plus exports	$54	$168

sales of agricultural products, mining products, manufactures, and freight receipts. The estimated total of moveable goods produced in the United States in 1964 was $280 billion.[11] There are technical reasons which make it improper to compare the $168 billion of sales abroad with $280 billion of domestic output of moveable goods. For example, a portion of our exports is shipped to United States-owned companies as components or semi-finished products. Thus, if we add such exports to output of United States-owned foreign business we are double counting. Adjusting for this and other sources of noncomparability, we arrive at a conservative estimate that the size of the foreign market (for domestic and United States-owned foreign firms) is equal to approximately two-fifths the domestic output of farms, factories, and mines.[12]

If this seems surprising to those who are accustomed to think in terms of Gross National Product, remember that the latter includes government expenditures, personal and professional services, trade, and activities of banks, real estate firms, and stock brokers. But as far as the business of farms, factories, and mines is concerned, foreign business amounts to quite a noteworthy volume relative to the internal market. Nor is this the whole story. These data do not include the considerable amount of sales abroad of foreign firms operating under copy-

---

* As defined by the Department of Commerce, direct investments are branch establishments or corporations in which United States firms own 25 percent or more of the voting stock.

** "Other investment" represents mainly stocks and bonds of foreign firms owned by United States firms and individuals.

right and patent agreements arranged by United States firms. As an example, one firm in the Philippines manufactures the following brand-name products under restricted licenses of United States firms: "Crayola" crayons, "Wessco" paints, "Old Town" carbon paper and typewriter ribbons, "Mongol" lead pencils, "Universal" paints, and "Parker Quink."

The Growing Importance of Foreign Economic Activity

The increasing relative importance of foreign economic activity is well illustrated by the experience of the manufacturing industries, as shown in Chart I and Table XXXIX. Here we compare total sales of domestic manufactures with exports of manufactures and sales of United States direct investments in foreign manufacturing activity. The data are plotted on a semi-logarithmic scale in the chart. Therefore, the narrowing of the distance between the two lines depicts the more rapid rise of the foreign market as compared with the growth of domestic markets.

CHART I

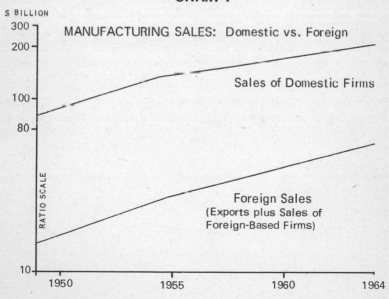

$ BILLION

MANUFACTURING SALES: Domestic vs. Foreign

Sales of Domestic Firms

Foreign Sales
(Exports plus Sales of
Foreign-Based Firms)

RATIO SCALE

300
200
100
80
10

1950   1955   1960   1964

TABLE XXXIX

MANUFACTURES
FOREIGN AND DOMESTIC SALES

(In Billions)

(1) Year	(2) Exports	(3) Sales by Foreign-based U.S. Firms	(4) Total Foreign Sales (2) + (3)		(5) Sales of Domestic Manufactures	
			Absolute	1950=100	Absolute	1950=100
1950	$ 7.4	$ 8.4	$15.8	100	89.8	100
1955	12.6	13.9	26.5	168	135.0	150
1960	16.1	23.6	39.7	251	164.0	183
1964	20.6	37.3	57.9	367	203.0	226

Source: Exports—U.S. Bureau of the Census, *Statistical Abstract of the United States: 1965*, pp. 877, 773. 1964 Sales of Domestic firms—U.S. Bureau of the Census, *Annual Survey of Manufactures, 1964*. Sales of foreign-based U.S. firms—the data for 1950 and 1955 are estimates based on the average relation between sales and investment abroad. (This is the procedure used by the National Industrial Conference Board.) Data for 1960 and 1964—*Survey of Current Business*, September 1962, p. 23, November 1965, p. 18.

Note: The data in columns (4) and (5) are not strictly comparable (see footnote 12.) However, the non-comparability does not destroy the validity of comparing the differences in the rates of growth of the two series.

Equally significant is the comparison of expenditures for plant and equipment in foreign-based and in domestic manufacturing firms (Chart II and Table XL). As in the preceding chart, the narrowing of the distance between the two lines is a clear portrayal of the increasing relative importance of business activity abroad. Expenditures for plant and equipment for United States subsidiaries abroad were a little over 8 percent of such expenditures of domestic firms in 1957. Last year this had risen to 17 percent.

CHART II

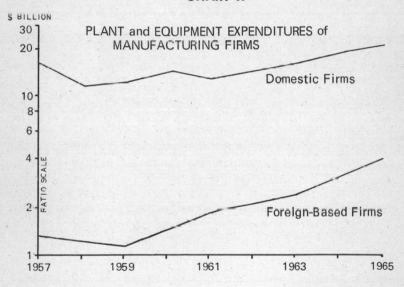

PLANT and EQUIPMENT EXPENDITURES of MANUFACTURING FIRMS

Domestic Firms

Foreign-Based Firms

TABLE XL
PLANT AND EQUIPMENT EXPENDITURES BY
U. S. DOMESTIC AND FOREIGN-BASED
MANUFACTURING FIRMS

| | Domestic Firms | | Foreign-Based Firms | | Foreign as |
Year	Billion $	1957=100	Billion $	1957=100	% of Domestic
1957	$16.0	100	$1.3	100	8.1
1958	11.4	71	1.2	92	10.5
1959	12.1	76	1.1	85	9.1
1960	14.5	91	1.4	108	9.7
1961	13.7	86	1.8	139	13.1
1962	14.7	92	2.0	154	13.6
1963	15.7	98	2.3	177	14.7
1964	18.6	116	3.0	231	16.1
1965	22.5	141	3.9	300	17.3

Source: Foreign-based firms—*Survey of Current Business,* September 1965, p. 28; September 1966, p. 30. Domestic firms—*Economic Report of the President,* Washington, D.C., 1966, p. 251.

It is not surprising to find, as shown in Chart III and Table XLI (pp.183,184), that profits from operations abroad are also becoming an ever more important component of business profits. In 1950, earnings on foreign investment represented about 10 percent of all after-tax profits of domestic nonfinancial corporations. By 1964, foreign sources of earnings accounted for about 22 percent of domestic nonfinancial corporate profits. In evaluating the significance of this we should also take into account (a) the understatement of foreign earnings because the latter do not include all the service payments transferred by foreign subsidiaries to home corporations, and (b) the financial advantages achieved in allocating costs between the home firms and foreign subsidiaries so as to minimize taxes. Moreover, we are comparing foreign earnings with earnings of all nonfinancial corporations—those that are purely domestic and those that operate abroad as well as in the United States. If we compared foreign earnings with total earnings of only those industries that operate abroad, the share of foreign earnings would of course be much larger than one fourth.

TABLE XLI

EARNINGS ON FOREIGN INVESTMENTS
AND DOMESTIC CORPORATE PROFITS

	Earnings on Foreign Investment	Profits (After Taxes) of Domestic Nonfinancial Corporations
	(Billions of Dollars)	
1950	2.1	21.7
1951	2.6	18.1
1952	2.7	16.0
1953	2.6	16.4
1954	2.8	16.3
1955	3.3	22.2
1956	3.8	22.1
1957	4.2	20.9
1958	3.7	17.5
1959	4.1	22.5
1960	4.7	20.6
1961	5.4	20.5
1962	5.9	23.9
1963	6.3	26.2
1964	7.1	31.3
1965	7.8	36.1

Source: Earnings on foreign investments—U.S. Department of Commerce, *Balance of Payments Statistical Supplement Revised Edition,* Washington, 1963; *Survey of Current Business,* August 1962, August 1963, August 1964, September 1965, June 1966, September 1966. Profits of nonfinancial domestic corporations— *Survey of Current Business,* September 1965, July 1966.

Note: Earnings include (a) earnings on direct investments abroad, (b) fees and royalties on direct investment transferred to parent companies in the U.S., and (c) income from "other" investments (other than direct) transferred to U.S. owners of these assets.

The significance of the last three tables is their representation of the rapid growth of the foreign sector. During the period when the economy as a whole was experiencing a slowing down in the rate of growth, foreign markets were an important source of expansion. For example, in manufacturing industries during the past ten years domestic sales increased by 50 percent, while foreign sales by United States-owned factories increased over 110 percent.

CHART III

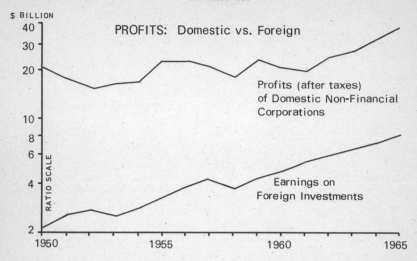

Thus, as far as the commodity-producing industries are concerned, foreign markets have become a major sphere of economic interest and have proven to be increasingly important to United States business as an offset to the stagnating tendencies of the inner markets.

This is quite obvious to American businessmen. The treasurer of General Electric Company put it this way in discussing "the need that American business has to keep expanding its foreign operations":

In this respect, I think business has reached a point in the road from which there is no turning back. American industry's marvelous technology and abundant capital resources have enabled us to produce the most remarkable run of peacetime prosperity in the nation's history. To keep this going, we have for several years sought additional outlets for these sources in foreign markets. For many companies, including General Electric, these offshore markets offer the most promising opportunities for expansion that we can see.[13]

It is also quite obvious that if foreign markets are so important to the commodity-producing industries, they are also of prime importance to the other interest groups, those whose profits and prosperity are dependent upon the welfare of the commodity-producers as well as those who benefit from servicing trade and investment in foreign markets: investment and commercial bankers, stock market speculators, transportation, insurance, etc.

Military Spending and Exports

For a full measure of economic involvement in foreign markets, the impact of military spending—the "defense" program—must also be reckoned with. The growth of our inner and outer markets has, since the founding of the Republic, been associated with the use (actual or threatened) of military force in peace as well as war. Professor William T. R. Fox states the case quite mildly: "The United States Army in peacetime was through most of the nineteenth century, extensively used to aid in the winning of the West, and especially in the suppression of Indian opposition to the opening up of new lands for settlement. Our Navy and Marine Corps, beginning with their exploits against the Barbary pirates were also engaged in making it safe for Americans to live and invest in remote places."[14]

While military activity is today presumably subordinated to national security needs, the "one-ness" of the national security and business interests persists: the size of the "free" world and the degree of its "security" define the geographic boundaries where capital is relatively free to invest and trade. The widespread military bases, the far-flung military activities, and the accompanying complex of expenditures at home and abroad serve many purposes of special interest to the business community: (1) protecting present and potential sources of raw materials; (2) safeguarding foreign markets and foreign investments; (3) conserving commercial sea and air routes; (4) preserving spheres of influence where United States business gets a competitive edge for investment and trade; (5) creating new foreign customers and investment opportunities via foreign military and economic aid; and, more generally, (6) maintaining the structure of world capitalist markets not only directly for the United States but also for its junior partners among the industrialized nations, countries in which United States business is becoming ever more closely enmeshed. But even all of this does not exhaust the "one-ness" of business interest and military activity, for we need to take into account the stake business has in the size and nature of military expenditures as a well-spring of new orders and profits.

As with exports, the significance of military spending for business and the economy as a whole is usually greatly under-estimated. One often hears that defense expenditures amount to less than 10 percent of the Gross National Product and that with a proper political environment comparable government spending for peaceful uses could accomplish as much for the economy. A crucial weakness of this approach is its un-critical acceptance of Gross National Product as a thing-in-itself. Because GNP is a useful statistical tool and one which has become entrenched in our ways of thought, we tend to ignore the underlying strategic relationships that determine the direction and degree of movement of the economic aggregates. Instead of examining the requirements of the industrial struc-ture and the dynamic elements of economic behavior, we tend to view the economy as blocks of billions of dollars that may be shifted at will from one column to another of the several cate-gories used by statisticians to construct the measurement of GNP.

To appreciate fully the critical influence of foreign markets and military expenditures on the domestic economy, recognition must be given to their exceptionally large impact on the capital goods industries. But first a comment on the capital goods in-dustries and the business cycle. There are diverse explanations of business cycles, but there can be no disputing the fact that the mechanics of the business cycle—the transmission mechan-ism, if you wish—is to be found in the ups and downs of the investment goods industries. There are cycles which are primarily related to the ebb and flow of inventories, but these are usually short-lived as long as the demand for investment goods does not collapse.

During a cyclical decline, the demand for consumer goods can be sustained for a period by several expedients such as unemployment relief, other welfare payments, and depletion of consumer savings. However, except for the most essential replacement needs, expenditures on investment goods theoretically can go down to zero. Businessmen naturally will not invest unless they expect to make a profit. The result of the diverse behavior of producer goods and consumer goods was classically demonstrated in the depression of the 1930's. During this probably worst depression in our history, purchases of consumer goods declined only 19 percent (between 1929 and 1933). Compare this with the behavior of the two major types of investment goods during the same period: expenditures for residential construction fell by 80 percent and nonresidential fixed investment dropped 71 percent.

With this as background, let us now focus on the post-Second World War relationship between (a) exports and military demand, and (b) a major category of investment, nonresidential fixed investment goods. Table XLII lists the industries producing nonresidential investment goods. It should be noted that a number of these industries also contribute to consumer goods (e.g., steel and machinery for autos) and to residential construction. This table presents the percentages of total demand (direct and indirect) created by exports and purchases of the federal government, which are almost entirely for military needs. These data are for the year 1958, the latest year for which there exists a complete input-output analysis for the United States economy.

As will be noted from Table XLII, in only one industry—farm machinery and equipment—did the combined export and military demand come to less than 20 percent of total demand. At the opposite extreme are the military industries par excellence—ordnance and aircraft. For all the other industries, the range of support given in 1958 by exports and military demand is from 20 to 50 percent.

While the available statistical data refer to only one year, the postwar patterns of exports and military expenditures suggest that this tabulation is a fair representation of the situation since the Korean War, and surely a gross underestimate during the Vietnam War. More information and study are required for a more thorough analysis. Meanwhile, the available

TABLE XLII

PERCENT OF TOTAL OUTPUT ATTRIBUTABLE TO EXPORTS AND FEDERAL PURCHASES, 1958

Industry	Percent of Output		
	Going into Exports	Purchased by Federal Government	Total of Exports and Federal Purchases
Iron and ferroalloy ores mining	13.5%	12.8%	26.3%
Nonferrous metal ores mining	9.1	35.6	44.7
Coal mining	19.1	6.3	25.4
Ordnance and accessories	1.7	86.7	88.4
Primary iron and steel manufacturing	10.1	12.5	22.6
Primary nonferrous metal manufacturing	10.1	22.3	32.4
Stamping, screw machine products	7.1	18.2	25.3
Other fabricated metal products	8.6	11.9	20.5
Engines and turbines	14.8	19.7	34.5
Farm machinery and equipment	10.0	2.9	12.9
Construction, mining and oil field machinery	26.9	6.1	33.0
Materials handling machinery and equipment	9.4	17.2	26.6
Metalworking machinery and equipment	14.0	20.6	34.6
Special industry machinery and equipment	17.5	4.3	21.8
General industrial machinery and equipment	13.4	15.3	28.7
Machine shop products	7.0	39.0	46.0
Electric industrial equipment and apparatus	9.8	17.0	26.8
Electric lighting and wiring equipment	5.5	14.5	20.0
Radio, TV and communication equipment	4.8	40.7	45.5
Electronic components and accessories	7.6	38.9	46.5
Misc. electrical machinery, equipment and supplies	8.9	15.1	24.0
Aircraft and parts	6.1	86.7	92.8
Other transportation equipment (not autos)	10.1	20.9	31.0
Scientific and controlling instruments	7.3	30.2	37.5

Source: "The Interindustry Structure of the United States," *Survey of Current Business*, November 1964, p. 14.

data warrant, in my opinion, these observations:

(1) Exports and military spending exert a distinctive influence on the economy because they fortify a strategic center of the existing industrial structure. This is especially noteworthy because business investment is not, as is too often conceived, a freely flowing stream. There is a definite interdependence between (a) the existing schedule of wage rates, prices, and profits, (b) the evolved structure of industry (the types of interrelated industries, each built to be profitable at the scale of obtainable domestic and foreign markets), and (c) the direction of profitable new investments. To put it in simpler terms, there are sound business reasons why investments flow in the direction they do and not in such ways as to meet the potential needs of this country—for example, to eliminate poverty, to provide the industry which would create equal opportunity to Negroes, to develop the underdeveloped regions of the United States, or create adequate housing. More important, business cannot invest to accomplish these ends and at the same time meet its necessary standards of profit, growth, and security for invested capital. Exports of capital goods and military demand flowing to the capital-goods producers, on the other hand, are uniquely advantageous in that they strengthen and make more profitable the established investment structure; they also contribute to an expansion of the industries that are most harmonious with and most profitable for the existing composition of capital.

(2) The support given by foreign economic involvement—both military and civilian commodities—makes a singular contribution by acting as a bulwark against the slippage of minor recessions into major depressions. It has accomplished this by shoring up one of the strategic balance wheels of the economy, the production of investment-type equipment—by supplying, as we have seen, from 20 to 50 percent of the market for these goods.

(3) We need also to take into account that it is *monopolistic* industry which dominates the volume and flow of investment and that such monopolistic businesses characteristically gear their investment policies to the "sure thing," where good

profits and safety of investment are reliably assured. Here the tie-in of government action and foreign policy is of paramount interest. The military-goods market usually has the decided advantage of supplying long-term contracts, often accompanied by enough guarantees to reduce and even eliminate any risk in building additional plant equipment, plant and equipment which may also be used for civilian purposes. In addition, military contracts pay for related research and development expenses, again removing risky aspects of normal investment programs. As for the foreign countries, the United States military presence, its foreign policy, and its national security commitments provide a valuable protective apparatus for the investments made in foreign markets. These foreign investments together with the demand created by governmental foreign aid, contribute importantly to the demand for the exports of the capital-goods and other manufacturing industries. The confidence in the consistency of government foreign policy and its complementary military policy can, and surely must, act as a valuable frame of reference for the domestic as well as foreign investment practices of monopolistic business.

(4)   The extra 20 to 50 percent of business provided by exports plus military demand (as shown for the key industries in Table XLII) provides a much greater percentage of the total profits of these firms. The typical economics of a manufacturing business requires that a firm reaches a certain level of productive activity before it can make a profit. Gross overhead costs— depreciation of machinery, use of plant, costs of administration— remain fairly constant at a given level of capacity. Until production reaches a point where at the market price of the final product enough income is produced to meet the overhead and direct costs, a business operates at a loss. Once this "break-even" point is reached, the profitability of the business surges forward until it hits against the limits of productive capacity. Of course the curve of profitability differs from industry to industry and from firm to firm. But the existence of a break-even point, and the upward swing of profits after the break-even point has been passed is a common characteristic of manufacturing industries. What this means is that for many of the

firms in the capital goods industries, the overlay of 20 to 50 percent of demand from military purchases and exports probably accounts for the major share of the profits, and in not a few firms perhaps as much as 80 to 100 percent of their profits.

Monopoly and Foreign Investments

One of the reasons frequently given for believing that economic imperialism is an unimportant influence in foreign and military policy is that only a small segment of American business is vitally concerned with foreign or military economic activities. This might be a meaningful observation if economic resources were widely distributed and the majority of domestic-minded business firms could conceivably be mobilized against policies fostered by the small minority of foreign-oriented businesses. But the realities of economic concentration suggest quite the opposite. In manufacturing industries, 5 corporations own over 15 percent of total net capital assets (as of 1962). The 100 largest corporations own 55 percent of total net capital assets.[15] This means that a small number of firms—with their own strength and that of their allies in finance and mass communication media—can wield an overwhelming amount of economic and political power, especially if there is a community of interest within this relatively small group.

And it is precisely among the giant corporations that we find the main centers of foreign and military economic operations. Just a cursory examination of the 50 largest industrial concerns shows the following types of firms heavily involved in international economic operations and the supply of military goods: 12 in oil, 5 in aviation, 3 in chemicals, 3 in steel, 3 in autos, 8 in electrical equipment and electronics, and 3 in rubber. These 37 companies account for over 90 percent of the assets of the top 50 industrial firms.

The community of interest among the industrial giants in foreign and military operations stems from relations that are not always obvious in terms of the customary statistical categories. First, there is the interrelationship among the firms via the financial centers of power. Second, there are the direct economic ties of business. While only five firms get one fourth of the volume of military contracts and 25 firms account for more than half of such contracts, a large part of this business is distributed to other businesses that supply these chief contractors.[16] Thus, as we saw in Table XLII the primary nonferrous metal manufacturers who receive very few direct military contracts nevertheless get over 22 percent of their business from military demand. And, third, because of the rich growth potential and other advantages of the military and foreign-oriented businesses, the postwar merger movement among industrial giants has intermingled the typically domestic with the typically outer-market directed business organizations. The most unlikely-seeming business organizations are today planted with both feet in foreign and military business. We see, for example, traditional producers of grain mill products and of plumbing and heating equipment acquiring plants that make scientific instruments; meat packing firms buying up companies in the general industrial machinery field, and many other cross-industry mergers.

The concentration of economic power, so much part of the domestic scene, shows up in even stronger fashion in the field of foreign investment. The basic available data on this are taken from the 1957 Census of foreign investments. (See table below.) These data refer only to direct investments and do not include portfolio investments or such economic ties as are

TABLE XLIII
U. S. DIRECT FOREIGN INVESTMENT
BY SIZE OF INVESTMENT (1957)

Value of Direct Investment by Size Classes	Number of Firms	Percent of Total U.S. Investment
$100 million and over	45	57
$ 50-100 million	51	14
$ 25- 50 million	67	9
$ 10- 25 million	126	8
$ 5- 10 million	166	5
Total	455	93

Source: *United States Business Investments in Foreign Countries*, U.S. Dept. of Commerce, 1960, p. 144.

created by the licensing of patents, processes, and trademarks. We note from this table that only 45 firms account for almost three fifths of all direct foreign investment. Eighty percent of all such investment is held by 163 firms. The evidence is still more striking when we examine the concentration of investment by industry:

Industry	No. of Firms	Percent of Total Assets Held
Mining	20	95
Oil	24	93
Manufacturing	149	81
Public Utilities	12	89
Trade	18	83
Finance and Insurance	23	76
Agriculture	6	83

These data are shown from the viewpoint of total United States foreign investment. If we examined the situation from the angle of the recipient countries, we would find an even higher degree of concentration of United States business activities. But from either perspective, the concentration of foreign investment is but an extension of domestic monopolistic trends. The latter provide the opportunity to accumulate the wealth needed for extensive foreign investment as well as the impetus for such investment.

The question of control is central to an understanding of the strategic factors that determine the pattern of foreign investment. In its starkest form, this control is most obvious in the economic relations with the underdeveloped countries— in the role of these countries as suppliers of raw materials for mass-production industries and as a source of what can properly be termed financial tribute.

Let us look first at the distribution of foreign investment as shown in Table XLIV. We see here two distinct patterns. In Latin America, Asia, and Africa, the majority of the investment is in the extractive industries. Although Canada is an important source of minerals and oil, only 35 percent of United States investment is in these extractive industries, with 45 percent going into manufactures. The investment in extractive industries

TABLE XLIV

PERCENT DISTRIBUTION OF DIRECT FOREIGN INVESTMENT BY AREA AND INDUSTRY, 1964

Industry	All Areas	Canada	Europe	Latin America	Africa	Asia	Oceania
Mining	8.0%	12.1%	0.4%	12.6%	21.9%	1.1%	6.3%
Petroleum	32.4	23.4	25.6	35.9	51.0	65.8	28.1
Manufacturing	38.0	44.8	54.3	24.3	13.8	17.5	54.1
Public Utilities	4.6	3.3	0.4	5.8	0.1	1.8	0.1
Trade	8.4	5.8	12.2	10.7	5.7	7.8	5.5
Other	8.6	10.6	7.1	10.7	7.5	6.0	5.9
Total	100.0	100.0	100.0	100.0	100.0	100.0	100.0

Source: Calculated from data in *Survey of Current Business*, September 1965, p. 24.

in Europe is minimal: the data on petroleum represent refineries and distribution, not oil wells.

The economic control, and hence the political control when dealing with foreign sources of raw material supplies, is of paramount importance to the monopoly-organized mass production industries in the home country. In industries such as steel, aluminum, and oil, the ability to control the source of raw material is essential to the control over the markets and prices of the final products, and serves as an effective safety factor in protecting the large investment in the manufacture and distribution of the final product. The resulting frustration of competition takes on two forms. First, when price and distribution of the raw material are controlled, the competitor's freedom of action is restricted; he cannot live very long without a dependable source of raw materials at a practical cost. Second, by gobbling up as much of the world's resources of this material as is feasible, a power group can forestall a weaker competitor from becoming more independent as well as discourage possible new competition. How convenient that a limited number of United States oil companies control two thirds of the "free world's" oil![17]

At this level of monopoly, the involvement of business interests with United States foreign policy becomes ever more close. The assurance of control over raw materials in most areas involves not just another business matter but is high on the agenda of maintaining industrial and financial power. And the wielders of this power, if they are to remain in the saddle, must use every effort to make sure that these sources of supply are always available on the most favorable terms: these foreign supplies are not merely an avenue to great profits but are the insurance policy on the monopolistic position at home.

The pressure to obtain external sources of raw materials has taken on a new dimension during the past two decades, and promises to become increasingly severe. Even though United States business has always had to rely on foreign sources for a number of important metals (e.g., bauxite, chrome, nickel, manganese, tungsten, tin), it has nevertheless been self-reliant and an exporter of a wide range of raw materials until quite recently. This generalization has been a mainstay of those who argued that U.S. capitalism had no need to be imperialistic. But even this argument, weak as it may have been in the past, can no longer be relied on. The developing pressure on natural resources, especially evident since the 1940's, stirred President Truman to establish a Materials Policy Commission to define the magnitude of the problem. The ensuing commission report, *Resources for Freedom* (Washington, D.C., 1952), graphically summarized the dramatic change in the following comparison for all raw materials other than food and gold: at the turn of the century, the U.S. produced on the whole some 15 percent more of these raw materials than was domestically consumed; this surplus had by 1950 turned into a deficit, with U.S. industry consuming 10 percent more than domestic production; extending the trends to 1975 showed that by then the overall deficit of raw materials for industry will be about 20 percent.

Perhaps the awareness of this development was a contributing factor to President Eisenhower's alerting the nation to the unity of political and economic interests in his first inaugural address (January 20, 1953): "We know . . . that we are linked to all free peoples not merely by a noble idea but by a simple need. No free people can for long cling to any privilege or enjoy any safety in economic solitude. For all our own material might, even we need markets in the world for the surpluses of our farms and our factories. Equally, we need for these same farms and factories vital materials and products of distant lands. This basic law of interdependence, so manifest in the commerce of peace, applies with thousand-fold intensity in the event of war."

As is so often the case, economic interests harmonize comfortably with political and security goals, since so many of the basic raw materials are considered essential to effective war preparedness. Quite understandably the government makes its contribution to the security of the nation as well as to the security of business via diplomatic maneuvers, maintenance of convenient military bases in various parts of the world, military aid to help maintain stable governments, and last but not least a foreign aid program which is a fine blend of declared hu-

manitarian aims about industrialization and a realistic appreciation that such progress should not interfere with the ability of
supplying countries to maintain a proper flow of raw materials.
To do a real job of assuring an adequate supply of raw materials in the light of possible exhaustion of already exploited
deposits, and in view of possible needs for missiles and space
programs, the government can make its greatest contribution
by keeping as much of the world as possible "free" and safe
for mineral development. Clarence B. Randall, president of
Inland Steel Co. and adviser on foreign aid in Washington,
comments on the fortunate availability of uranium deposits in
the Belgian Congo as the atom bomb was developed: "What
a break it was for us that the mother country was on our
side! And who can possibly foresee today which of the vast
unexplored areas of the world may likewise possess some unique
deposit of a rare raw material which in the fullness of time our
industry or our defense program may most urgently need?"[18]

The integration of less developed capitalisms into the world
market as reliable and continuous suppliers of their natural resources results, with rare exceptions, in a continuous dependency
on the centers of monopoly control that is sanctified and ce-
mented by the market structure which evolves from this very
dependency. Integration into world capitalist markets has almost uniform effects on the supplying countries: (1) they de-
part from, or never enter, the paths of development that
require independence and self-reliance; (2) they lose their
economic self-sufficiency and become dependent on exports for
their economic viability; (3) their industrial structure becomes
adapted to the needs of supplying specialized exports at prices
acceptable to the buyers, reducing thereby such flexibility of
productive resources as is needed for a diversified and growing
economic productivity. The familiar symptom of this process
is still seen in Latin America where, despite industrialization
efforts and the stimulus of two world wars, well over 90 percent
of most countries' total exports consists of the export of agricultural and mineral products.[19] The extreme dependence on
exports, and on a severely restricted number of export products
at that, keeps such economies off balance in their international
economic relations and creates frequent need for borrowing.

Debt engenders increasing debt, for the servicing of the debt adds additional balance of payments difficulties. And in all such relations of borrowing and lending, the channels of international finance are in the hands of the foreign investors, their business associates, and their government agencies.

The chains of dependence may be manipulated by the political, financial, and military arms of the centers of empire, with the help of the Marines, military bases, bribery, CIA operations, financial maneuvers, and the like. But the material basis of this dependence is an industrial and financial structure which through the so-called normal operations of the marketplace reproduces the conditions of economic dependence.

A critical element of the market patterns which helps perpetuate the underdeveloped countries as dependable suppliers of raw materials is the financial tribute to the foreign owners who extract not only natural resources but handsome profits as well. The following comparison for the years 1950-1965 is a clear illustration of the process and refers to only one kind of financial drain, the income from direct investments which is transferred to the United States: [20]

		(Billions of Dollars)		
	Europe	Canada	Latin America	All other Areas
Flow of direct investments from U.S.	$8.1	$6.8	$3.8	$5.2
Income on this capital transferred to U.S.	5.5	5.9	11.3	14.3
Net	+$2.6	+$ .9	−$ 7.5	−$ 9.1

In the underdeveloped regions almost three times as much money was taken out as was put in. And note well that besides drawing out almost three times as much as they put in, investors were able to increase the value of the assets owned in these regions manifold: in Latin America, direct investments owned by United States business during this period increased from $4.5 to $10.3 billion; in Asia and Africa, from $1.3 to $4.7 billion.

The contrasting pattern in the flow of funds to and from Europe indicates a post-Second World War trend. The rapid growth of investment in Europe was in the manufacturing and oil refining fields. The developments in foreign investment in manufacturing are closely related to the normal business drive to (a) control markets and (b) minimize costs of production. The methods used will vary according to the industry and the conditions in each country. The main factors involved in relying on capital investment instead of relying on export trade are:

(1) If the profit rate obtainable by manufacturing abroad is greater than by increasing domestic production.

(2) If it facilitates getting a larger and more secure share of a given foreign market.

(3) If it enables taking advantage of the channels of export trade of the country in which investment is made. Thus, United States business firms in England account for 10 percent of Britain's exports.[21]

(4) If it is possible to pre-empt a field of industry based on new technological developments, usually protected by exercise of patent rights. But the most dramatic development of our times is the spread of United States industry into the computer, atomic energy, and space technology activities of industrialized countries. The rapid spread of these fields is motivated, to be sure, by immediate profit opportunities. But it most likely also has the aim of helping to maintain, and get full advantage of, the technical edge United States business now has as a result of the vast investment made by the United States government in research and development. The dominant position in this technology may be decisive in achieving wider control of the rest of the economy, when and if the new technology becomes the key to the productive forces of a society.

Such investment as is made by United States capital in manufacturing in underdeveloped countries occurs primarily in Latin America, where the percentage of total United States investment in the field of manufacturing is 24 percent. This investment is mainly in light manufacturing industry, including the processing of native food materials. Manufacturing operations in the durable goods field, such as autos, takes the form of assembly plants. This guarantees the export market of components and parts. It also contributes to stabilizing the market for these United States products. It is much easier for a country faced with severe balance of payments difficulties to prohibit imports of a luxury product than to eliminate the import of raw materials and assembly parts which will create unemployment and shut down local industry.

The postwar foreign economic expansion of United States manufacturing firms has resulted in the transformation of many of the giants of United States business into a new form of multinational organizations. The typical international business firm is no longer limited to the giant oil company. It is as likely to be a General Motors or a General Electric—with 15 to 20 percent of its operations involved in foreign business, and exercising all efforts to increase this share. It is the professed goal of these international firms to obtain the lowest unit production costs on a world-wide basis. It is also their aim, though not necessarily openly stated, to come out on top in the merger movement in the European Common Market and to control as large a share of the world market as they do of the United States market. To the directors of such organizations the "oneness" of economic and national interests is quite apparent. The president of General Electric put it succinctly: "I suggest we will perceive: that overriding both the common purposes and cross-purposes of business and government, there is a broader pattern—a 'consensus' if you will, where public and private interest come together, cooperate, interact and become the national interest."[22]

Needless to stress, the term "private interest" refers to private enterprise. Another officer of this corporation grapples with the identity of the private and national interest: "Thus, our search for profits places us squarely in line with the national policy of stepping up international trade as a means of strengthening the free world in the Cold War confrontation with Communism."[23]

Just as the fight against Communism helps the search for profits, so the search for profits helps the fight against Com-

urces of non-comparability arise from (a) the estimated $168 bil-
udes sales of trade organizations, public utilities, and other non-
ity producers, and (b) the data on sales of domestic manufactures
 value-added basis while the sales of foreign affiliates are on a
shipments basis. Conservative estimates of adjustments to obtain
bility reduce the $168 billion to $110 billion.

John D. Lockton, "Walking the International Tightrope," address
nal Industrial Conference Board, May 21, 1965, published by
Electric Co., Schenectady, N. Y., 1965, pp. 4-5.

William T. R. Fox, "Military Representation Abroad," in The
tation of the United States Abroad, a report of The American
, Graduate School of Business, Columbia University, New York,
. 124-125.

Hearings, Subcommittee on Antitrust and Monopoly of the Com-
 the Judiciary, U.S. Senate, 88th Congress, 2nd Session, Part I,
on, D.C., 1964, p. 115.

Background Material on Economic Aspects of Military Procure-
 Supply: 1964, Joint Economic Committee of Congress, Washing-
., 1964, p. 11.

A. George Gols, "Postwar U.S. Foreign Petroleum Investment,
ond F. Mikesell, ed., U.S. Private and Government Investment
University of Oregon Books, Eugene, Oregon, 1962, p. 417.

Clarence B. Randall, The Communist Challenge to American
Little Brown & Co., Boston, 1959, p. 36.

Joseph Grunwald, "Resource Aspects of Latin American Develop-
 Marion Clawson, ed., National Resources and International De-
t, Johns Hopkins Press, Baltimore, 1964, p. 315.

These are summations of data presented for 1950 to 1960 in
artment of Commerce, Balance of Payments Statistical Supple-
vised Edition, Washington, D.C., 1963. The data for 1961 to
ear in the review articles on foreign investment in various issues
rvey of Current Business from 1962 to 1966. The first line in
table represents net capital outflows of direct investment from
d States. The second line is the sum of dividends, interest, and
rofits, after foreign taxes, produced by direct investments abroad.
ot include the earnings of corporate subsidiaries (as distinguished
nches) which are retained abroad.

John H. Dunning, American Investment in British Manufacturing
 London, 1958.

Speech by Fred J. Borch, President of General Electric Com-
Our Common Cause in World Competition," before The Economic
New York, November 9, 1964, printed by General Electric Co.,
ady, N. Y.

Speech by John D. Lockton, Treasurer of General Electric Com-
e Creative Power of Profits," at Macalester College, St. Paul,
pril 22, 1964, printed by General Electric Co., Schenectady, N. Y.

munism. What more perfect harmo
imagined?

NOTES

1. American Board of Commissioners f
nual Report (1841), as quoted in Richard
American Empire, Chicago, Quadrangle B
originally published in 1960 by Oxford U
highly recommended for a better unders
United States foreign policy. See also Cl
National Interest, reissued in 1966 by Qu
material; and Lloyd C. Gardner, *Econom
plomacy,* Madison, University of Wisconsin
2. *Niles' National Register,* January 2
3. Foreword to Samuel Lubell, *The F
American Economic Policy,* New York, Har
4. *International Security—The Militar*
of the Special Studies Project of Rockefelle
N.Y., Doubleday & Co., 1958, p. 24.
5. The full title reads, *The United
Asset—What the Navy has done for Indu*
the Office of Naval Intelligence, U.S. Nav
lished in 1923 by the U.S. Government Pri
The following excerpt is typical: "In the A
is kept on constant patrol in the Yangtse
patrol from the mouth of the river up n
heart of China. American businessmen hav
United States withdraw this patrol they w
time. Our Navy not only protects our own
is constantly protecting humanity in ge
engages the bands of bandits who infest thi
6. Eugene R. Black, *The Domestic
Columbia Journal of World Business,* Vol.
7. Address by Assistant Commerce Sec
meeting of the Tax Foundation, Inc., as re
December 5, 1965.
8. Richard D. Robinson, *International I
Rinehart and Winston, 1966, p. 220.
9. *Economic Considerations in Foreign
Alfred Wentworth* in *Political,* Vol. I, No.
10. *The Conference Board Record,* Vo
See also Judd Polk, Irene W. Meister and I
tion Abroad and the Balance of Payments:
ment Experience, New York, National Indu
11. This total consists of (a) cash
plus consumption of farm products in the fa
in manufacturing industries, (c) value of
freight receipts.
12. The Department of Commerce est
ports was shipped to foreign affiliates of U

APPENDIX A

U.S. Defense Commitments and Assurances

A List of Treaties and Official Declarations in Effect in 1966

Western Hemisphere

Treaties

1. Inter-American Treaty of Reciprocal Assistance (Rio Pact), September 2, 1947.
2. Applicability of North Atlantic Treaty, April 4, 1949 (NATO applies to Canada, Iceland, Greenland, Bahamas, Bermuda).
3. Bilateral Agreements
   a. Agreement with Denmark concerning the defense of Greenland, April 27, 1951.
   b. Defense agreement with the Republic of Iceland, May 5, 1951.
   c. North American Air Defense Command Agreement (exchange of notes, U.S.-Canada, May 12, 1958).
   d. Treaty with Panama, March 2, 1936.

Official Declarations

1. Seventh Annual Message of President Monroe to Congress (the Monroe Doctrine), December 2, 1823.
2. Statement by the Department of State on the continued applicability of the Monroe Doctrine, July 14, 1960.
3. The Ogdensburg Agreement (with Canada—setting up a Permanent Joint Board of Defense), August 18, 1940.
4. Joint Announcement on Defense, U.S.-Canada, February 12, 1947.
5. Joint Statement by President Kennedy and President Betancourt of Venezuela, February 20, 1963 (U.S. pledges full support to Venezuela).

Europe

Treaties

1. North Atlantic Treaty, April 4, 1949. Parties to the treaty: United States, Belgium, Canada, Denmark, France, Iceland, Italy, Luxembourg, Netherlands, Norway, Portugal, United

Kingdom, Greece (added 1952), Turkey (added 1952), Federal
Republic of Germany (added 1955).
2. Joint Declaration concerning the Renewal of the Defense Agreement of September 26, 1953, U.S.-Spain, September 26, 1963.

Official Declarations

1. Statement by President Eisenhower on U.S. policy towards
   Western European Union, March 10, 1955.
2. Communique, North Atlantic Council Ministerial Session, Athens,
   May 6, 1962.
3. Final Act, London Nine-Power Conference, Declaration by the
   Governments of the U.S., United Kingdom, and France, October
   3, 1954.
4. Statement by President Kennedy regarding Berlin, July 25, 1961.
5. Address by Vice-President Johnson before the West Berlin
   House of Representatives, August 19, 1961.
6. Statement by Secretary of State Rusk regarding Berlin, February
   22, 1962.
7. Joint Communique, President Kennedy and Chancellor Adenauer
   of Germany, November 15, 1962.
8. Joint Communique, President Johnson and Chancellor Erhard
   of Germany, June 12, 1964.

Near East — Middle East

Treaties

1. Applicability of North Atlantic Treaty since 1952 (on February
   18, 1952, Greece and Turkey acceded to the North Atlantic
   Treaty; since that date they have been covered by the commitments of that Treaty).
2. U.S. membership in CENTO Committees (the Pact of Mutual
   Cooperation—Baghdad Pact—between Iraq, Turkey, United
   Kingdom, Pakistan, and Iran was signed February 24, 1955.
   This was later renamed Central Treaty Organization—CENTO,
   after Iraq withdrew. The U.S. is a member of the Military,
   Economic, and Anti-Subversion Committees of CENTO and an
   observer at Council meetings).
3. Bilateral Agreements
   a. Agreement of Cooperation with Iran, March 5, 1959.
   b. Agreement of Cooperation with Turkey, March 5, 1959.

Official Declarations

1. Message of President Truman to Congress (the Truman Doctrine), March 12, 1947.
2. Joint Resolution to Promote Peace and Stability in the Middle
   East (the Eisenhower Doctrine), March 9, 1957.
3. Tripartite Declaration (U.S.-United Kingdom-France) regarding
   Security in the Near East, May 25, 1950.
4. Multilateral Declaration respecting the Baghdad Pact, (U.S.
   commitments to Pakistan, Iran, and Turkey), July 28, 1958.

5. Joint Communique, President Kennedy and the Shah of Iran, April 13, 1962.
6. Letter from President Kennedy to Crown Prince Faisal of Saudi Arabia, October 25, 1962.
7. Statement on Jordan and Saudi Arabia by Secretary of State Rusk, March 8, 1963.
8. Reply by President Kennedy to a news conference question concerning the Middle East, May 8, 1963.
9. Remarks of President Johnson during Exchange of Toasts with President Shazar of Israel, August 2, 1966.

Africa

Treaties

1. Agreement of Cooperation with Liberia, July 8, 1959.

South Asia

Treaties

1. United States membership in CENTO committees (same as above under Near East-Middle East).
2. Membership in SEATO (see Treaties under Southeast Asia-Southwest Pacific).
3. Agreement of Cooperation with Pakistan, March 5, 1959.

Official Declarations

1. Letter from President Eisenhower to Prime Minister Nehru of India, February 24, 1954.
2. Assurances to Pakistan respecting extension of military assistance to India: Statement by Department of State, November 17, 1962.

Southeast Asia — Southwest Pacific

Treaties

1. Southeast Asia Collective Defense Treaty, September 8, 1954 (SEATO is the resulting organization, which includes U.S., Australia, France, New Zealand, Pakistan, Philippines, Thailand, United Kingdom, Cambodia, Laos, South Vietnam).
2. Security Treaty between Australia, New Zealand, and the U.S. (ANZUS Pact), September 1, 1951.
3. Mutual Defense Treaty with Philippines, August 30, 1951.

Official Declarations

1. Tonkin Gulf Resolution, August 10, 1964.
2. Joint Communique, Secretary Rusk and Foreign Minister Thanat Khoman of Thailand, March 6, 1962.
3. Declaration of Honolulu, February 8, 1966.
4. Joint Communique, President Johnson and Philippine President Macapagal, October 6, 1964.

East Asia

Treaties

1. Treaty of Mutual Cooperation and Security between U.S. and Japan, January 19, 1960.
2. Mutual Defense Treaty with the Republic of China (Formosa), December 2, 1954.
3. Mutual Defense Treaty with the Republic of Korea, October 1, 1953.

Official Declarations

1. Joint Resolution Authorizing the President to Employ the Armed Forces of the United States for Protecting the Security of Formosa, the Pescadores and Related Positions and Territories of that Area (Formosa Straits Resolution), January 29, 1955.
2. Statement on Formosa and the offshore Islands by President Kennedy in a Press Conference, June 27, 1962.
3. Reply to Question at Press Conference in Korea by Vice President Humphrey, February 23, 1966.

Source: Compilation presented by State Department on U.S. defense commitments and assurances as of August 1966. *Hearing before Preparedness Investigating Subcommittee of Committee on Armed Services,* United States Senate, 89th Congress, 2nd Session, August 25 and 30, 1966.

APPENDIX B

U.S. Involvement in International Political Crises and Critical Situations, 1961 to Mid-1966 (I)

1. Vietnamese struggle with Viet Minh and Viet Cong (1945-   )—Partial (from 1950) to direct (from 1954) involvement as supplier of military assistance, military advisers, then combat troops at the request of the Republic of Vietnam.

2. Berlin (1948-   )—Direct involvement as one of four occupying powers under 1945 quadripartite agreements.

3. Communist Chinese threat to Formosa Straits (1950-   )—Direct involvement under Truman (1950) and Eisenhower (1953); instructions to U.S. Seventh Fleet and Formosa Resolution (1955).

4. Korea (1950-   )—Direct involvement as a principal contributor of forces under UN Command during Korean War and to present.

5. Bay of Pigs episode (1961)—Direct involvement as unofficial, partial protector of invasion force.

6. Panamanian-United States dispute over conditions in and administration of the Canal Zone (1962-1966)—Direct involvement as a party to the dispute; OAS and UN action; bilateral negotiations.

7. Cuban missile crisis (1962-1963)—Direct involvement as power enforcing OAS quarantine on shipment of missiles to Cuba.

8. Cambodian complaint of border violations by U.S. and South Vietnamese forces (1964-   )—Direct involvement as a party named in the complaint; UN action.

9. Stanleyville (Congo) rebel mistreatment of European prisoners (1964)—Direct involvement in bringing matter to UN attention and in providing airlift for Belgian para-commando rescue mission.

10. Dominican crisis (1965-1966)—Direct involvement through initial action to stabilize the situation; contributor to OAS peace forces.

---

(1) This list does not include temporary crises brought about by coup d'etat (e.g. the Syrian Army coup of 1962) or by internal rebellions (e.g. the revolt of the Kurds in Iraq in 1962).

Source: This is a reproduction of Part A of a Statement submitted by Secretary of State to the U.S. Senate Committee on Armed Services. Worldwide Military Commitments, Hearings Before the Preparedness Investigating Subcommittee of the Committee on Armed Services, U.S. Senate, 89th Congress, 2nd session, August 25 and 30, 1966, Part I, pp. 31 and 32.

This statement also contained a list of 27 other crises in which U.S. involvement was indirect, such as supplying arms or cooperating in UN actions. This list is given on p. 32 of the above source.

MONTHLY REVIEW

an independent socialist magazine

edited by Paul M. Sweezy and Harry Magdoff

Business Week: ". . . a brand of socialism that is thorough-going and tough-minded, drastic enough to provide the sharp break with the past that many left-wingers in the underdeveloped countries see as essential. At the same time they maintain a sturdy independence of both Moscow and Peking that appeals to neutralists. And their skill in manipulating the abstruse concepts of modern economics impresses would-be intellectuals. . . . Their analysis of the troubles of capitalism is just plausible enough to be disturbing."

Bertrand Russell: "Your journal has been of the greatest interest to me over a period of time. I am not a Marxist by any means as I have sought to show in critiques published in several books, but I recognize the power of much of your own analysis and where I disagree I find your journal valuable and of stimulating importance. I want to thank you for your work and to tell you of my appreciation of it."

The Wellesley Department of Economics: " . . . the leading Marxist intellectual (not Communist) economic journal published anywhere in the world, and is on our subscription list at the College library for good reasons."

Albert Einstein: "Clarity about the aims and problems of socialism is of greatest significance in our age of transition. . . . I consider the founding of this magazine to be an important public service." (In his article, "Why Socialism" in Vol. I, No. 1.)

DOMESTIC: $9 for one year, $16 for two years, $7 for one-year student subscription.

FOREIGN: $10 for one year, $18 for two years, $8 for one-year student subscription. (Subscription rates subject to change.)

62 West 14th Street, New York, New York 10011